PARIS
past and present

Texts
Milena Ercole Pozzoli

Editing Supervision
Valeria Manferto De Fabianis

Graphic design
Patrizia Balocco

Graphic layout
Anna Galliani
Alberto Bertolazzi
Clara Zanotti

Translation
Neil Frazer Davenport

1 In this unusual shot, the Eiffel Tower is framed between the obelisk from Luxor and one of the many statues that grace the famous Place de la Concorde.

2-3 An aerial view of the Seine, the celebrated river flowing through Paris along the banks of which the city's intense trading activities were concentrated up until the end of the 17th century.

CONTENTS

This edition published by
Barnes & Noble Publishing, Inc.,
by arrangement with
White Star S.p.a.,
2005 Barnes & Noble Books

M1098765432
ISBN-13:978-0-7607-7381-9
ISBN 0-7607-7381-5

Library of Congress
Cataloging-in-Publication
Data available

Color separations by Fotomec, Turin
Printed in Indonesia

ANCIENT GLORIES, NEW SPLENDORS

There are many things that each dawn change the face of Paris and ensure that it is, and always will be, one of the world's most talked-about cities. Almost as if by divine right, there has been no other capital that has had such a dominant influence over the rest of its country and Europe as Paris. Since the 6th century, when Clovis chose it as the capital of Gaul, Paris has never wavered from this consecrated path. Knowing how to project continuously its broad and mutating appeal has long been a particular talent. Paris has always been able to renew its creative energy in infinite celebration of its own myth and is always adept at finding ways of talking about itself, through music, theater, painting, cinema, literature, and architecture. The Eiffel Tower was built in celebration of the centennial of the French Revolution; Pompidou decided to link his name with that most controversial urban planning project, the bizarre Beaubourg. In his turn, Mitterrand backed the Grand Arche de la Défense project and celebrated the bicentennial of the founding of the Louvre with the opening of a new wing of the museum pierced by the tip of a glass pyramid, projecting light into the subterranean labyrinth of the Cour Napoléon. He also authorized the building of the immense National Library: four skyscrapers standing like vast books of concrete and glass, open to the sky.

Paris is a city of continual challenges and movement, bold in its imposition of the contagious youthfulness of the most excessive of avant-garde projects, and at the same time a grande dame ever capable of provocation and seduction. But Paris is above all a state of mind, an imaginary world, a great unspoiled dream, a living legend that conquers

4–5 *The top of the Eiffel Tower offers an uninterrupted panorama in all directions. On clear days the whole city is visible and the most important monuments can be easily identified. In the photograph at the top, the shadow of the famous Iron Lady is cast on the Seine, from the Arc de Triomphe to the Basilica of the Sacré-Coeur. The photograph on the bottom left shows the white Sacré-Coeur rising from the celebrated slopes of Montmartre. Lastly, in the photograph on the right, the golden light of sunset enhances the grandiose Palais Chaillot.*

with its sudden hold over the senses. It is a capital of the world and of the spirit.

Most visitors come to Paris on the pretext of finding out what is new in order to be reassured that the old is unchanged, and it is on the subtle boundary between past and present that they find the uniqueness of this metropolis. In contrast with other capitals, Paris blends its past and future: the 17th-century quarters and the Défense, the Louvre treasure chest and the challenge of the glass pyramid, the great boulevards and the heavily criticized Opéra-Bastille. If there is a city in the world that can claim to have been a cradle of the avant-garde, that city is Paris. Here were born the most violent of political, cultural, artistic, and social revolutions, from the Reformation to the can-can, from Cubism to the civil unrest of 1968, from fashion to architecture to the cinema. Almost all the writers and painters who count, from the mid-19th century onward, have lived and dreamed in Paris; no other city in the world can claim as much.

Brilliant and adventurous people have lived on every street corner, have inhabited Bohemian attics and sumptuous palaces, have wept, laughed, loved, suffered, and, above all, written chapters, exposed miles of celluloid, sculpted faces, and painted canvases that have become pages in the very history of the city itself. It was here that Stendhal wrote, in just 52 days, *La Chartreuse de Parme*; Picasso lived and worked; and Modigliani found a house in Rue Delta in Montmartre and later in Montparnasse. In the church of Saint-Roch, Alessandro Manzoni saw the light and decided on his conversion; Casanova lodged in Rue de Tournon; Goldoni died in Rue Dussoubs; and Chopin drew his last

6 *Paul Jouve's sculptures of a bull's head and a dog, the gilding glittering in the sun, adorn the Trocadero Fountain.*

6–7 *This stunning photograph, taken from the Arc de Triomphe, shows Paris as the sun sets.*

8–9 *The Pont Alexandre III is a Parisian jewel, gilded and grandiose in accordance with the seductive stylistic canons of the Belle Époque. No fewer than 17 artists worked on its decoration, and the foundation stone was laid by Tsar Alexander II, although it was his successor who saw the completion of the great work and to whom it was dedicated in a solemn inauguration ceremony in 1900.*

10–11 *When it was erected it was a source of scandal, but more than 100 years later, the Eiffel Tower, an attraction built for the 1889 World's Fair, is so much a part of the Parisian landscape as to be the symbolic hub around which the whole city revolves. In this image, the Iron Lady appears to be rising from the roofs of the city.*

breath in a white palace near Place Vendôme.

Paris is the city where reality and literature have always met, as if in the suspended universe of a dream. The streets are roamed by the ghosts of authors and by the spirits of characters that came into the world through the authors' pens, spirits that carry with them a world of pure imagination. They go in and out of houses, they wander the banks of the Seine, linger in the yellow lamplight of Parisian nights, and whisper among the lime trees of St-Germain-des-Prés. They, too, are an integral part of the atmosphere of Paris, along with a sensation that the city is holding something special in store, an adventure, a surprise, a favor, an emotion. From the city's faded rooftops, dotted with chimneys, from the romantic parks, from the top of the Eiffel Tower, or from a stroll along the bridges of the Seine, Paris reveals the myriad facets of its popularity and offers the fullness of its appeal to tourists and residents alike. Although Paris retains its mysteries and is the ideal city of folly, it is also a futuristic capital of telecommunications, a city that lives according to frenetic rhythms and exploits every last square inch of space, a city of the ephemeral and exorbitant prices. After all, what modern metropolis does not exist through perennial contradictions?

The difference is that Paris possesses the exclusive weapon of total seduction and unconsciously infects us all with its eternal and irrepressible joie de vivre.

12–13 *An evocative aerial photograph of the old street plan and the principal monuments of Paris. The Ile de la Cité and the Ile St-Louis, the historic heart of the city, are clearly visible.*

1 ARC DE TRIOMPHE
2 PALAIS CHAILLOT
3 EIFFEL TOWER
4 GRAND PALAIS
5 PLACE DE LA CONCORDE
6 MUSÉE D'ORSAY
7 ASSEMBLÉE NATIONALE
8 LES INVALIDES
9 MONTPARNASSE
10 INSTITUT DE FRANCE
11 PALAIS DE JUSTICE ET SAINTE-CHAPELLE
12 SÉNAT

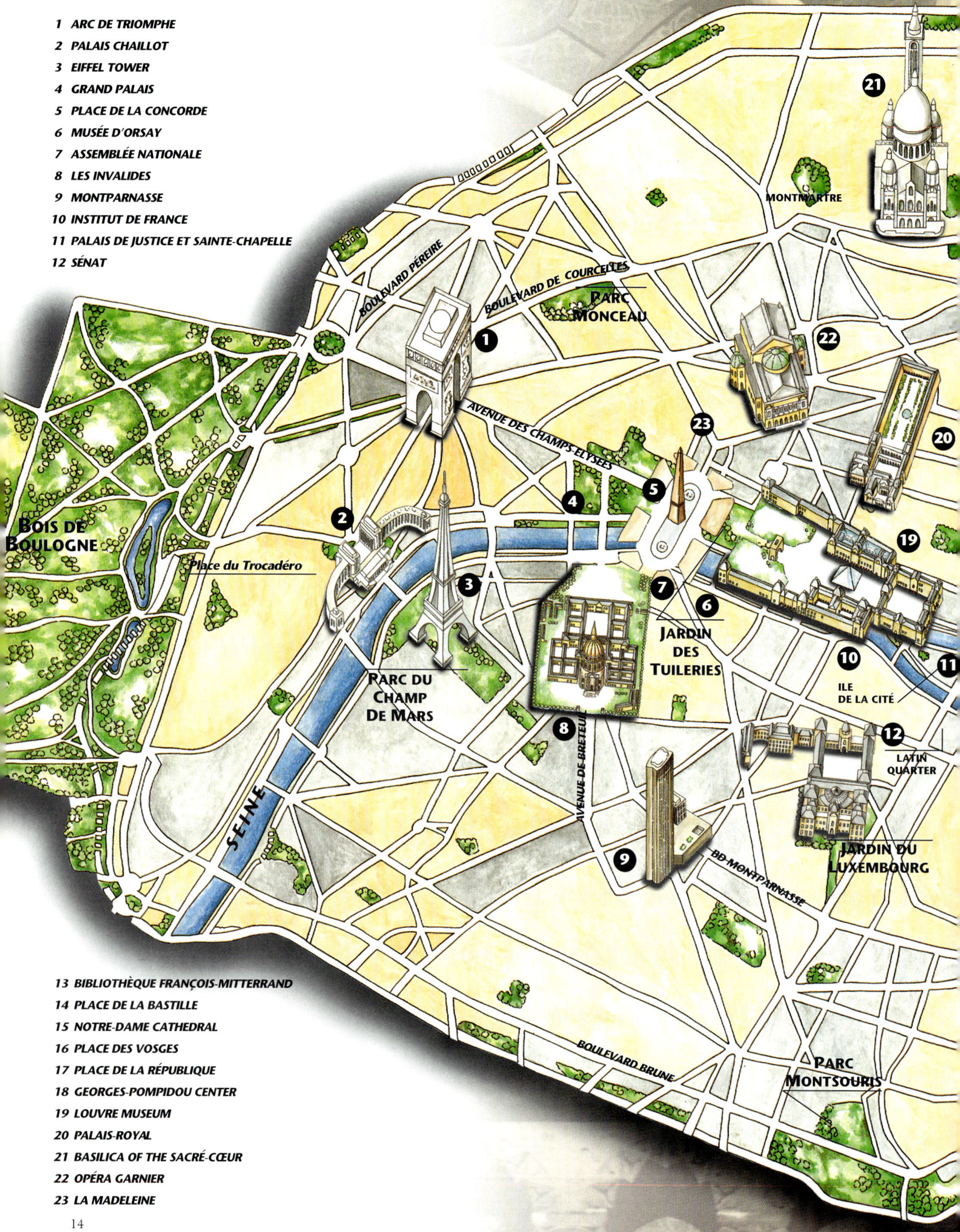

13 BIBLIOTHÈQUE FRANÇOIS-MITTERRAND
14 PLACE DE LA BASTILLE
15 NOTRE-DAME CATHEDRAL
16 PLACE DES VOSGES
17 PLACE DE LA RÉPUBLIQUE
18 GEORGES-POMPIDOU CENTER
19 LOUVRE MUSEUM
20 PALAIS-ROYAL
21 BASILICA OF THE SACRÉ-CŒUR
22 OPÉRA GARNIER
23 LA MADELEINE

PARC DE LA VILLETTE
BOULEVARD ROCHECHOUART
PARC DES BUTTES CHAUMONT
NAL ST-MARTIN
BOULEVARD ST-DENIS
BOULEVARD DE BELLEVILLE
PÈRE-LACHAISE CEMETARY
17
BOULEVARD BEAUMARCHAIS
16
8
15
LE SAINT LOUIS
14
SEINE
JARDIN DES PLANTES
Place de la Nation
13
BOULEVARD VINCENT AURIOL

ETERNAL GRANDEUR

16–17 *Reproduced in the works of Julius Caesar and Strabone, the antique street plan of Roman Lutetia shows the primitive nucleus of the nascent city created on the Ile de la Cité in the Seine. The extensive flood plain was still completely forested.*

Jewels, vases, furnishings, necklaces, axes, daggers, and statuettes have been recovered during archaeological excavations in Paris over the past 200 years. The artifacts have allowed scholars to reconstruct the decisive phases in the development of Paris. The legendary Roman *oppidum* has revealed many of its secrets: the location of the principal streets; the foundations of the forum; the remains of the *capitolium*; the theater; and the arena. In Bercy, the 13th arrondissement, the construction of an underground parking lot unearthed a Neolithic village, a number of wooden canoes, and 250 Bronze Age vases; excavations along the Rue Pierre-et-Marie-Curie uncovered a Gallic-Roman kiln found almost intact; and the subsoil of Notre-Dame has given up, the pillars of the Temple of Tiberius, erected on behalf of the boatsmen's guild in the middle of the 1st century BC.

Digs around the Latin Quarter have also helped to complete the picture of ancient Lutetia, the Gallic-Roman village built on the foundations of the primitive village inhabited by the Parisii tribe. In the year 52 BC, one of Julius Caesar's centurions arrived to challenge the Gaul Camulogenus near this settlement, which was composed of simple huts on an island in the middle of the Seine. The full-scale war that followed led to the destruction of the Gauls. The Roman settlement of Lutetia was then raised on the remains of the ancient village on the cradle-shaped island now known as the Ile de la Cité. The principal axis was oriented along the approximate route of what is today Rue St-Jacques and probably led straight to the boats moored along the banks of the Seine.

16 top left
Over the centuries the birth of Paris has inspired engravings, prints, paintings, and bas-reliefs. This illustration shows part of ancient Lutetia, taken from an engraving published in Paris à Travers les Siècles, *by historian G. de Genouillac.*

16 bottom left and top right
The first inhabitants of what in time was to become the legendary Ville Lumière were the Parisii, a rough, primitive people. These engravings show men and women engaged in daily chores.

17 top
Paris à Travers les Siècles, *by G. de Genouillac, published in 1878, depicts the early Gauls and the horsemen of the 1st century AD who inhabited what was to become Paris.*

18 top
Every epoch has produced historical figures who have contributed to the history and legend of Paris. In 250, the first bishop, St. Denis, hated by the pagan priests who are depicted in this manuscript in the act of dispatching messengers to Rome to ask for help against him, died a martyr on what was to become the famous hill of Montmartre.

This was, for all intents and purposes, the birth of Paris. "The gravel beach of that island was its first city wall, the Seine its first moat" wrote Victor Hugo in *Notre-Dame de Paris.* He went on to add, "For a number of centuries Paris remained an island, with two bridges, one to the north, the other to the south and two bridgeheads that served her as both ports and fortresses, the Grand-Châtelet on the right bank and the Petit-Châtelet on the left. Then, from the epoch of the kings of the first dynasty, Paris, feeling constrained on her island on which there was no longer space in which to move, decided to cross the river. Beyond the larger and smaller Châtelets a first turreted wall of stone began to enclose the countryside on either side of the Seine... little by little the tide of houses, thrust out from the heart of the city toward the periphery, broached, eroded and erased that first wall." The sequence of civil wars and the barbarian invasions did little to prevent Rome from extending its control for many centuries over these lands and much of France.

In 250, the first bishop, St. Denis, died as a martyr on, as legend would have it, the hill that would later become known as Montmartre, but Christianity nevertheless spread through the small community. From

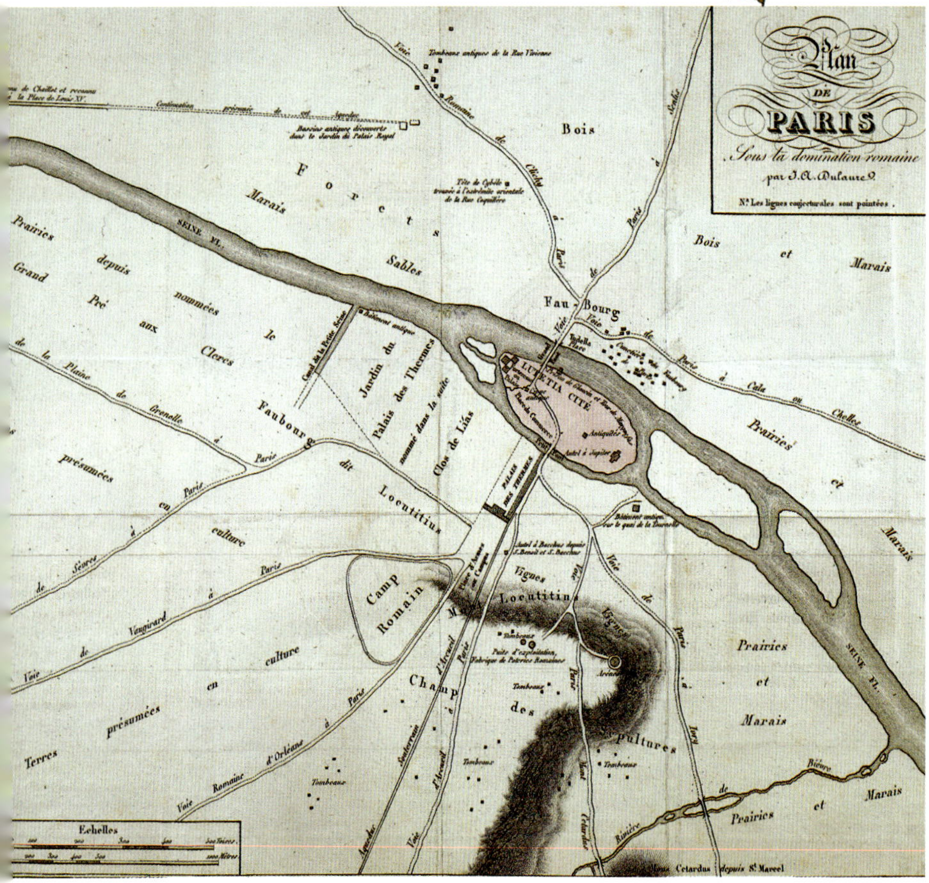

18 bottom
Many areas of Paris have provided traces of the ancient Roman oppidum *with the principal* cardum, *or axis, that perhaps led directly to the boats moored along the banks of the river. Archaeological investigations have reconstructed the development of Paris from an insignificant Neolithic village to the glorious* Ville Lumière. *Every excavation has added pages to the centuries-long story of this fantastic city. From one arrondissement to the next, every open building site offers an opportunity for a fascinating trip through time.*

19 left
The first of a series of barbarian raids by the tribes from beyond the Rhine occurred in 275. Faced with this threat, Paris retreated within the fortified Cité. Attila, the Scourge of God, as noted in this illustration taken from a 12th-century painting, besieged the city in 451.

19 right
Legend has it that because of the divine intervention sought by the young Geneviève, seen here in an illustration by Lion Royer from Le Petit Journal, *the fearsome Attila departed for the south without sacking the city.*

275 onward the threat of barbarian invasions represented a severe test of the defences of the *oppidum*. In the 4th century, the already densely populated fortified city was protected by the fleet of Roman ships moored on the Seine, a small but well-armed garrison, and massive city walls. For more than a century, the houses clambered one on top of the other, and the streets became increasingly narrow, imprisoned within the ring of tall, solid towers. In the 5th century, Paris stubbornly resisted a siege by Attila the Hun, backed by the divine intervention of young Geneviève, who convinced the besieged population to pray. As if by a miracle, Attila's army turned around and headed south, leaving the city untouched. Lutetia, by now known as Paris, was safe, and Geneviève was later canonized and proclaimed the patron saint of the city. A slim, pale marble statue of Geneviève dominates the Pont de la Tournelle.

20 top
These helmeted and armored warriors from the era of the alliance between the Franks and the Gauls give an idea of the customs and costumes of Merovingian Paris. Soon after he was declared king, Clovis transferred the capital of his kingdom to the banks of the Seine.

20 center left
Victorious at Soissons over the troops of the Roman Empire, Clovis (481–511) became master of Gaul, converted to Roman Catholicism, and was proclaimed king of the Franks and crowned in Reims cathedral, as can be seen here in an illustration taken from Les Grandes Chroniques de France.

20 center right
Taken from Paris à Travers les Siècles, *this engraving shows Clovis being carried in triumph by his men.*

Late in the 5th century, the history of the Salian Franks was unified with that of Roman Gaul. Clovis, victorious at Soissons against the troops of the Roman Empire, became king of Gaul. He married the Christian Clotilda, who persuaded him and his army to convert to her religion. He was crowned king of the Franks (from whom the name of the country derives) at Reims in 481 and transferred the capital of his kingdom to the banks of the Seine.

During this period, Paris was dotted with half-built churches: there were nine in construction on the left bank and three on the right. Clovis ordered the construction of a church dedicated to the Apostles where he wished to be buried and where, some time later, the remains of St. Geneviève were also interred. A son, Childebert, who was to reign for 47 years, commissioned the building on the same bank of the Seine of an immense basilica, the largest in Merovingian Gaul, and another that housed the remains of St. Germain, the bishop of Paris late in the 6th century, on the foundations of which the St-Germain-des-Prés abbey was built.

20 bottom
This illustration from 1541 depicts the coronation of King Pepin by St. Boniface in 751.

21 top
Charlemagne briefly resided in Paris, preferring Rome or Aix-la-Chapelle to the city on the Seine. In this painting by Julius Schorr von Carlosfeld he is seen entering Paris in triumph.

21 bottom left
In 751, after he deposed Childeric III (the last Merovingian king), Pepin the Short was crowned king. Pepin's son, Charlemagne, succeeded him. Charlemagne is seen here in regal dress and with the symbols of power in his hands in a celebrated portrait by Albrecht Dürer. The king subsequently left Paris defenseless, and late in the 9th century, the city was sacked on a number of occasions by the Normans. The Cité resisted a long siege, but nothing remained of the Roman Paris of the Rive Gauche.

21 bottom right
A 15th-century engraving of the Ile de la Cité in the era of Charlemagne. The city was already notably well developed.

The Merovingians conquered almost all Roman Gaul, but with the advent of the 7th century, civil disorder, the undisciplined court life, the lack of a political policy, the division of the kingdom, and internal strife among the rulers led to the decay of the dynasty and the rise of Pepin the Short and the Carolingians. In 751, the last Merovingian king, Childeric III, was deposed by Pepin, who took the title of king. When Pepin's son, Charlemagne, came to the throne, he established the capitals of his kingdom at Rome and Aix-la-Chapelle and was rarely resident in Paris. Hard times began when the city was abandoned by the last of the Carolingians, and during the 9th century, it was sacked by Norman adventurers. The outskirts were destroyed and as Paris retreated within the confines of the Cité the last traces of the Roman *oppidum* disappeared.

22 top left *The accession to the throne of the Capetians, from the left, Hugh Capet, Robert, and Constance, restored Paris to its role as the capital of the kingdom and the center of power. The city expanded, and trading in textiles with Flanders and in fish with the north led to the development of the Rive Droite.*

22 top right *Louis VI "the Large" (1108–1137), depicted visiting a building site in an engraving from the 14th century, established his residence in the palace on the Ile de la Cité, an island crowded with houses and workshops.*

22–23 *By the year 1000, Paris was a large, flourishing city, as this engraving of the street plan of medieval Paris testifies.*

23 top *Blanche of Castile, the wife of Louis VIII, was responsible for the construction of the celebrated Gothic Sainte-Chapelle.*

23 right *After Philip II (1179–1223) came to the throne, work began on a massive new defensive wall around the city.*

In 987, Hugh Capet of the Capetian dynasty was crowned king, and, as it approached its first millennium, Paris resumed its role as capital of the kingdom. Louis VI "the Large" (1108–1137) established his residence in a palace on the Cité, the original island, which was increasingly crowded with houses. In 1163, Bishop Maurice de Sully began the construction of Notre-Dame on the site of the old Merovingian church, and in 1180, Philip II enclosed the city in a new ring of fortified walls with tall, powerful towers. To protect himself from the assaults of the king of England, Philip built the Louvre fortress, which soon served as a royal residence and gave new support to Les Halles de Champeaux, the celebrated Paris market established by Louis the Large that remained in situ for eight centuries. Blanche of Castile, wife of Louis VIII, commissioned the building of Sainte-Chapelle. After a few decades the new city walls were too small to allow for the expansion of the city that was by now composed of 14 parishes.

Medieval Paris developed on the right bank of the Seine and was a major center on the great trading and communications routes. Textiles from Flanders arrived along Rue St-Denis, grain along Rue St-Honoré, and fish from Normandy and Brittany arrived in the city along Rue des Poissoniers. The Seine, the most natural and

immediate means of transportation for trade, was by now the scene of a constant bustle of barges and boats. "The houses breached the walls of Philip Augustus," wrote Victor Hugo, "and happily scattered across the plain with neither order nor symmetry as if they had escaped from a prison. Once there they dug a garden in the fields and sat at their ease."

Parisian suburbs began to develop during this period and are linked to the expansion of the inhabited areas around the first urban parishes, such as St-Germain l'Auxerrois, St-Merry, St-Jacques-la-Boucherie, and St-Nicolas-des-Champs. In contrast, the left bank was almost completely abandoned. The slopes of the Ste-Geneviève hill were owned by the monks of the great abbeys, such as the nearby and already flourishing St-Germain-des-Prés, and were used for agricultural purposes.

Under St. Louis IX, the aristocracy was weakened by the crusades in the Holy Land and against the Cathars. The city's university, instituted and recognized by a Papal Bull issued in 1209 by Pope Innocent III, ensured that Paris enjoyed international prestige as a center of learning. In 1257, Robert de Sorbon founded a university for the teaching of theology, law, art, and medicine. When he came to the throne, Charles V ordered the construction of the Bastille and city walls on the right bank to enclose the new quarters. Once again, however, the walls soon proved inadequate in the face of the city's continued rapid expansion. By the 15th century, Paris extended far beyond the concentric rings of fortifications that since the era of Julian the Apostate had attempted to restrain the city within their defenses.

24 left
St. Louis IX, visiting Notre-Dame accompanied by his mother, Blanche of Castile. According to Jacques Le Goff, "he was a sainted knight, a sainted warrior. The king applied the two great rules of Christian war, of right and just war, whilst continuing to serve the interests of the French monarchy." St. Louis attempted to be an ideal Christian king, whose virtues were manifested through power, wisdom, and goodness.

24 right
St. Louis in front of the Church of John the Baptist. In the background are the towers of Paris.

25 *Charles V, "the Wise," in a portrait by Orley Bernard, was an able financial strategist and skillfully reorganized the army. Having reopened the war with the English, he managed to reduce their possessions to a few coastal fortresses. While he was still the dauphin, he had had to tackle the first Parisian revolt led by Etienne Marcel, the spokesman for a discontented populace. Charles came to the throne after the execution of Marcel and carried with him the memory of those signals of fracture between sovereign power and the capital. His first act as king was to leave the Ile de la Cité (top left), order the building of the Bastille, and complete the construction of a new city wall on the right bank that, following the course of the Seine, was set at a right angle to the present-day Carrousel. Charles also began the meticulous transformation of the Louvre (bottom) from a fortress to a royal palace. He had the building heightened, enriched with windows, decorated with statues, and embellished internally. He placed his rich library in the northwest court and his collection of works of art in the large halls. He also ordered the planting of lush gardens with porticoes and pavilions.*

26 top
The elder son of Edward II and Isabella of France, Edward III, depicted here in regal dress, married Philippa of Hainaut and acceded to the English throne at a very early age after the deposition of his father. Because of his youth, Parliament nominated a regency council to advise him, but his mother and her lover, Roger Mortimer, usurped power. The couple's bad government led to a new regency council that banished the queen to Castle Rising and executed Mortimer. After the death of Charles V, Edward III claimed the throne of France. The struggle between the Capetians and the English sovereign gave rise to the Hundred Years War in 1337.

The 14th century was a difficult period for Paris. In 1348, the city was struck by the Black Death, a plague that killed 200,000 people. Even worse, the ongoing struggle for the French throne between the Capetians and the English king Edward III of the Plantagenet dynasty sparked off the Hundred Years War (1337–1453). The one positive outcome of the war was that it brought to an end a series of civil disorders provoked by legendary demagogues such as Simon Caboche and Capeluche, who threw Paris into a climate of terror between 1413 and 1418. After the death of Charles VI, the dauphin and future king, Charles VII, fled the peril of rebellion and sought refuge at Bourges. During the period of his gilded exile, the banks of the Loire, with their enchanted castles, were adopted as the "capital" of the kingdom. The English entered Paris in 1422, after the death of Charles V, and proclaimed Henry VI of England the king of France, despite his youth. Just as victory appeared to be within the English

grasp, a country girl, Joan of Arc, reached the French army and implored the Capetian king, Charles VII, who was staying at Chinon, to allow her to march at the head of his troops. The enemy was routed, and Charles VII entered Paris in triumph and was crowned king. Joan of Arc was accused of witchcraft and burned to death by the English, who eventually left French soil in 1453.

26 bottom
A 15th-century miniature of a battle between knights on horseback during the Hundred Years War. The English occupation, the devastation caused by the war, and the economic crisis all had an effect on Paris. In 1348, the city was also struck by the Black Death, which decimated the population.

27 left
Joan of Arc, the legendary Maid of Orléans, fighting in front of the St-Honoré gate. Legend has it that she was sent by God to restore Charles VII, who was hiding at Chinon to avoid the perils of the capital, to the throne of France. Joan of Arc arrived in Chinon on March 9, 1429, to be presented to the king. When she was introduced to him, she said, "My name is Joan, I have been sent by the King of the Heavens to tell you that you will be crowned as the true king of the French in the cathedral of Reims."

27 right *In this contemporary miniature, Charles VII is seated upon the French throne, surrounded by members of his court.*

30 top *Niece of Lorenzo the Magnificent, daughter of the duke of Urbino, Lorenzo de' Medici, and the French princess Madeleine d'Auvergne, and mother of three kings of France, Catherine de Médicis (in a painting depicting her in her youth) had one of the most remarkable lives in history. In a century of both splendor and horror, she was educated in Florence, but at a very early age was sent to France to marry Henry of Orléans, the son of Francis I. The king never loved her and openly preferred throughout his life his lover, Diane de Poitiers. But Catherine, in spite of being despised as a foreigner and not of royal blood, was in a certain sense queen for 30 years, because she was the mother of three kings of France, who succeeded one another. Her life was often in danger, but she confronted every threat with courage.*

30–31 *The St. Bartholomew's Day massacre happened on August 24, 1572. This incident, in which thousands of Huguenots (French Protestants) were killed, is depicted here in a famous painting by François Dubois.*

31 top right
An engraving of the events that took place on May 12, 1588, when the capital was barricaded and violent clashes took place over religious differences.

31 left
This fresco by Giorgio Vasari in the Sala Regia of the Vatican portrays a scene of the St. Bartholomew's Day Massacre, in particular its justification by Charles IX to the Parliament.

This was the era in which Rabelais, a Franciscan monk, attacked monks, the church, princes, and politics from his priory near Tours, and Calvin was attracting proselytes for his Reformation. In Paris, the first to be infected by these new ideas were wealthy merchants, princes, and intellectuals. The Wars of Religion and political infighting broke out quickly, and in 1572, the Huguenots were massacred in Paris on St. Bartholomew's Day. It was a difficult moment for France, and the Huguenot king, Henry IV, who to enter Paris and save his throne was obliged to convert to Roman Catholicism. The king passed into history with the celebrated phrase "Paris is well worth a Mass" in 1594. Having assumed power, Henry restored the city and elevated it from a ruin to an ideal urban civilization. At the threshold of the Grand Siècle, Descartes stirred debates among the intellectuals of the western world, and Place Dauphine and Place des Vosges, the first great royal squares, were completed.

31 bottom right
To secure the French crown, Henry IV converted to Catholicism. After his coronation, he restored the ruined city, embellishing it with new works, opening the first large squares, and reviving work on the Louvre and the Tuileries. He also inaugurated the Pont-Neuf and encouraged the development of the Marais and the urbanization of the Ile St-Louis. He also commissioned Place des Vosges, initially as a plaza for equestrian competition, but aristocrats soon arrived to live in the sumptuous redbrick buildings surrounding the square.

32 left
The king of France and Navarre, Louis XIII (above), portrayed in a famous contemporary painting, made Paris a grand capital, taking the initiative on many projects, but above all leaving Cardinal Richelieu, here depicted in his official gowns, free to construct the Palais Cardinal, today the Palais-Royal.

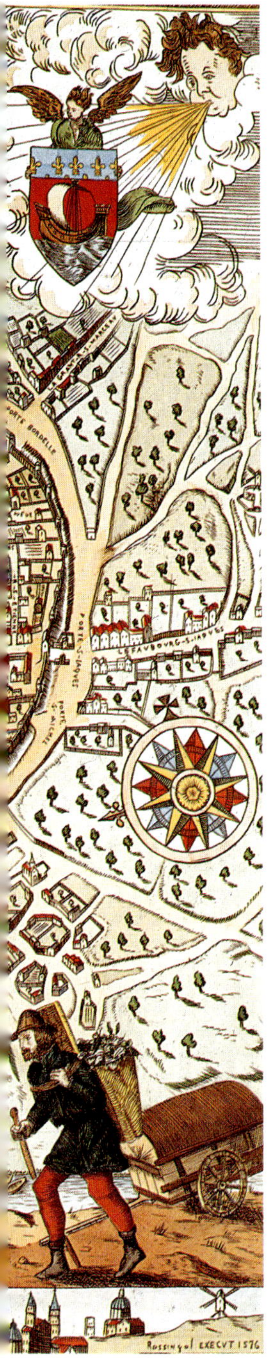

32–33 and 32 bottom *By the 17th century Paris had expanded in all directions. This map of the city and the print dating from that period clearly depict the expansion and the urban agglomeration locked inside the city's massive circular walls.*

33 *The city continued to grow. Above is an extraordinary view of the Louvre and the Seine from the Pont-Neuf; the painting in the center offers a view of the Louvre; and the painting below shows the Seine from the Ile de la Cité. During this period, architect Louis Le Barbier was creating a new quarter on the left bank between the university and the Seine, and Christophe Marie was building on the two muddy, uninhabited islands bordering the Ile de la Cité.*

After the reign of Louis XIII (1610–1643), which was dominated by the controversial figure of Cardinal Richelieu, the future Louis XIV (1643–1715), the author of the famous phrase "I am the State," came to throne at just five years of age. He replaced the old city walls of Paris with great boulevards, promoted the creation of extensive public parks, and built the grandiose Palace of Versailles. The Sun King transferred his court to his magnificent new palace in 1682.

The Sun King was succeeded by Louis XV (1715–1774), who also lived at Versailles and devoted himself to the embellishment of Paris, by now a city of about 500,000 inhabitants. He united the Faubourg St-Honoré with the Faubourg St-Germain and the Pont-Royal, and had more bridges constructed over the Seine. He also ordered that the ancient Cemetery of Sts-Innocents, a source of infection and disease, be demolished and replaced by a great market. The Panthéon, the École Militaire, and the Place de la Concorde were also improved. On the international political front, the disastrous Seven Years War (1756–1763) concluded with the loss of the colonies in Canada, the West Indies, and India to the British, and the capital, in the absence of the king, increasingly became a hotbed of revolutionary ideas.

34 *In 1500, Paris was experiencing a moment of glory and architectural reconstruction, but it was also devastated by the Wars of Religion, aggravated by the Fronde activities that turned Louis XIV against the city (the Sun King is portrayed below with drawings for the royal residence spread out on the table). In spite of Louis XIV's obsession with the Palace of Versailles, splendidly depicted above, the city began to assume an appearance that is recognizable today. Sixty convents were built in the first decades of the 17th century. Colbert, the controller of the finances and the superintendent of the monuments of the capital, ensured that during the reign of Louis XIV Paris saw the construction of many new buildings, including the Observatory and the Hôtel Royal des Invalides. The latter was designed by Hardouin-Mansart, a great architect and friend of the king who complied with and interpreted Louis XIV's desire to construct the immense Palace of Versailles.*

35 top and bottom left
Although absorbed by Versailles, Louis XV did not forget the Tuileries (above), to which continuous modifications were made. Great staircases, galleries, and new apartments were built, and the garden, with its flowerbeds and fountains, where noblemen and ladies would step aside as the king passed, became one of the most felicitous spaces of the grandiose construction.

35 bottom right
During the 17th century, Paris became ever more beautiful around the Tuileries. These images show a glimpse of the Seine and Notre-Dame (above) and a view of the port near the Tour St-Jacques (below).

36 left
Historical events have made Louis XVI (portrayed above in his coronation outfit) and Marie-Antoinette of Austria (bottom, in a painting by Elisabeth-Louise Vigée-Lebrun) the most famous sovereigns in French history. She was the youngest and favorite of the 15 children of Emperor Francis I and Maria Theresa of Austria. When she was only 10 years old, she was promised as the wife of the dauphin of France, who was then only 12.

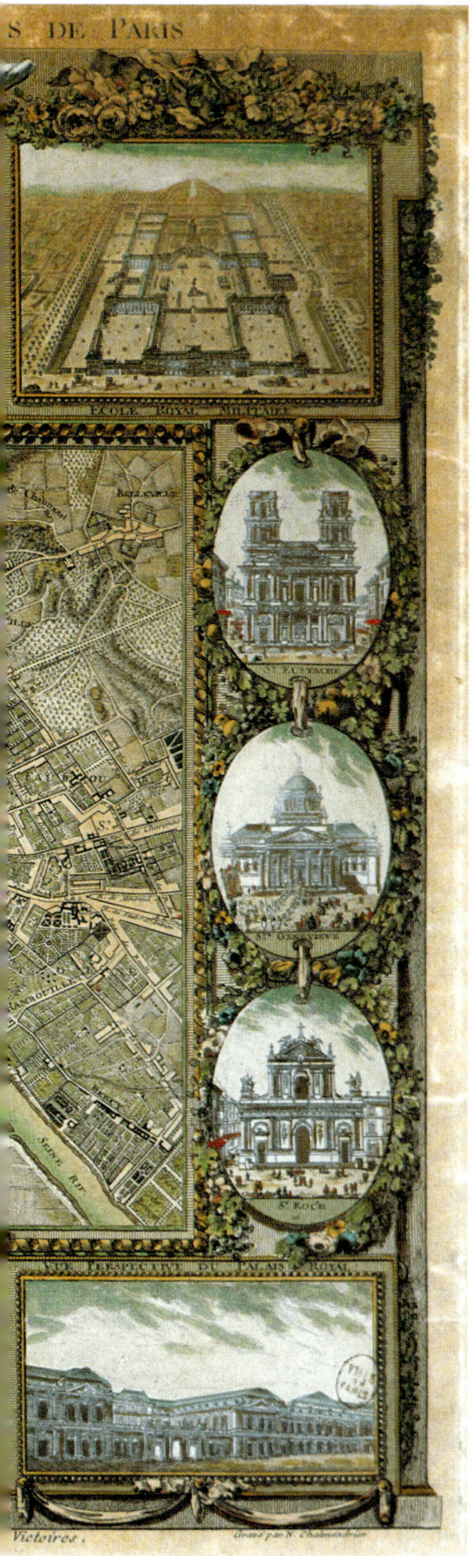

In an atmosphere that was by now hostile to the crown, Louis XVI came to the throne in 1774 with his Austrian wife, Marie-Antoinette. On the May 5, 1789, the States General met at Versailles in a climate of expectation, convinced that radical changes were on the horizon. After the elaborate opening ceremony, and before tackling the real problems, the assembly was faced with a major procedural question of whether the motions presented should be voted according to order or per head. The representatives of the Third Estate (the upper and middles classes), numerically superior to the other two orders together (the nobility and the clerics), were in favor of voting per head. The other two orders preferred to vote per order because this would ensure them secure victory and confirm their privileges. The question seemed insoluble until the Third Estate suddenly proclaimed its own National Assembly in a surprising and significant move. Intervention by the king was in vain, and the privileged orders were obliged to bow to the will of the bourgeoisie and agree terms. On July 9, 1789, the National Assembly was proclaimed the Constituent Assembly and the States General ceased to exist. The king still hoped to regain control of the situation by dismissing liberal minister Necker and ordering a strong garrison to be placed around Versailles.

36–37 *This map shows the development of Paris between 1785 and 1789.*

37 *While Marie-Antoinette was squandering huge sums, the people were being infected by new revolutionary ideas.*

On May 5, 1789, the States General met at Versailles (top) in a climate of expectation. This meeting was the first the first signal of the Revolution. The painting below shows the famous Jeu-de-Paume speech on June 20, 1789.

38 top
The storming of the Bastille, the symbolic event that sparked off the revolution, in a print from the period. It was followed by another fundamental event, the Declaration of the Rights of Man, which today can be admired in a room of the Musée Carnavalet. These immortal principles echoed throughout Europe.

The revolution was triggered on July 14, 1789, when the people, exasperated by a sharp rise in the price of bread and inflamed by revolutionary ideas, flooded the streets and squares and besieged the prison, the symbol of royal despotism. The storming of the Bastille had as an immediate consequence the constitution of a new municipal council, the Commune, which immediately replaced the old aristocratic administrators with members of the bourgeoisie and decided upon the constitution of an urban militia, known as the National Guard, under La Fayette. A revolutionary wind blew throughout France. After the Declaration of the Rights of Man, the situation continued to escalate. On June 20, 1791, Louis XVI escaped from the Tuileries, where he had been obliged to reside after leaving Versailles, and attempted to reach the troops faithful to him in Lorraine. He was recognized at Varennes, arrested, and brought back under escort to Paris. Imprisoned in the Temple Tower, he was put on trial, condemned to death, and executed on January 21, 1793.

The French Revolution had profound echoes throughout Europe. Goethe predicted as much upon the victory of the Jacobin volunteers over

39 top left
The protagonists of the revolution inspired many artists. This image shows La Fayette at the Champs-de-Mars on July 14, 1790.

39 bottom left
The Musée Carnavalet contains many relics of the French Revolution, such as the symbol of the revolt as represented by the legendary phrase "Liberté, Egalité, Fraternité"

39 top right
After the revolution, the royal family left Versailles and returned to Paris. They were imprisoned in the Tuileries and later executed at the Place de la Concorde. In this painting, Louis XVI is being accompanied to the gallows on January 21, 1793.

39 bottom right
Marat, the French revolutionary who in 1789 began publication of the newspaper L'Ami du Peuple, *is carried in triumph. His articles against the Assembly had a significant impact upon the course of the revolution. He was one of the most active Montagnards (those who sat on the high benches in the Assembly) and president of the Jacobin Club. In this capacity he conducted an open war against the Girondins. He was eventually assasinated by the knife of Charlotte Corday.*

the Austrians and Prussians at Valmy on September 20, 1792: "From this place and from this day begins a new era in the history of the world."

38 bottom
The Proclamation of the Rights of Man was heard as a new gospel that would lead to the liberation and regeneration of all men. The work of disciples of the philosophers, and apparently addressing all the populace, the Declaration of Rights clearly revealed its bourgeois origins and was full of restrictions and conditions. Civil rights were conceded to all French citizens. Protestants and Jews were granted the right of citizenship, slavery was abolished in France but not in the colonies, and political rights were reserved for a minority.

40 top left
Napoléon in full dress uniform, an ermine cloak, and a laurel wreath of solid gold.

40 top right
Napoléon's farewell to his troops and his abdication on April 20, 1814.

40–41 *This famous painting by Jacques-Louis David shows the most solemn moment in the life of Napoléon Bonaparte, when he crowned himself emperor of the French in the Cathedral of Notre-Dame. The scene is worthy of a king. Napoléon is dressed in a brocade tunic embroidered with golden bees and an ermine-lined cloak. After his coronation, he crowned his wife, Josephine Beauharnais, under the gaze of Pope Pius VII. Later, despite his sincere love for his wife, he was to disown her when she was unable to provide a heir.*

After the revolution, internal difficulties forced the country to seek new wars instead of peace. Early in 1796, the Directory planned a grand offensive against the Habsburgs. At the head of the army charged with restraining the Austrian troops in Italy while two other French units were attacking Austria from the German side was Napoléon Bonaparte. A dark, bitter, and wild character, Napoléon had some of the haughtiness and rebelliousness of a Corsican bandit (he was born in Ajaccio in 1796), but his military and political career was brilliant and unstoppable. After his return from the French campaign in Egypt, he was appointed first consul. In 1804, in the presence of the pope, he crowned himself emperor in Notre-Dame. The setting was magnificent, worthy of a royal coronation, and Napoléon wore an embroidered gold tunic and was wrapped in an ermine-lined cloak decorated with golden bees. Four dignitaries were needed to help him support his costume. The famous Pitt diamond was set in the grip of his sword, and on his head was a precious crown of laurels glittering with diamonds—the work of Biennais, the court jeweller, and costing 8,000 francs.

The coronation signalled the beginning of the legend of the great Corsican. The emperor declared war against half of Europe, defeated the Austrians at Austerlitz, descended into Italy, and then confronted the terrible Russian winter with the dream of deposing the tsar. Napoléon's epic invasion ended in catastrophe. In March 1814, the allies conquered Paris: Russians, Prussians, Cossacks, and Austrians marched down the Champs-Élysées. Napoléon abdicated and left for the island of Elba. The Congress of Vienna consigned the throne of France to the Bourbons, but in March 1815 Napoléon escaped from Elba, landed in the south of France, and marched upon Paris. His "100 days" finished at Waterloo: He was defeated by the British and exiled to the remote island of St. Helena in the middle of the Atlantic Ocean, where he died in 1821.

41 *Two episodes of Napoléon's military campaign: Russian troops encamped upon the Champs-Élysées on March 31, 1814 (top), and the entry of the allied powers into Paris (bottom).*

42 top
The revolution left Paris with no significant monuments apart from the grand patriotic space of the Champs-de-Mars. Sacking and confiscations took place in this period, and vast estates belonging to religious orders or members of the aristocracy were liberated and passed into the hands of new speculators. The Commission of Artists was formed to give new order to the city plan, but with no great results. When he became first consul, Napoléon affirmed that "if Paris is to be beautified, there is more to demolish than to construct. Why not knock down the whole quarter of the Cité, that vast ruin fit to house only rats?" As emperor he could realize his dream of making Paris the most beautiful city in the world. He opened Rue de Rivoli and had the market of Les Halles reorganized. Four bridges were built across the Seine, the arch on the Carrousel was constructed, and the colossal Arc de Triomphe on the Étoile was begun. The Palais du Luxembourg, seen here, became the home to the senate under Napoléon.

42 center and bottom
Napoléon's grand innovative and revivalist plans for the rebirth of Paris included the completion of La Madeleine, center, which resembles a Greek temple. Napoléon housed his veteran soldiers at the Hôtel des Invalides (bottom).

42–43 *The Panthéon, in a famous painting depicting it in the mid-19th century, houses the tombs of the most illustrious figures of France.*

43 top *These two illustrations present two celebrated Paris churches: St-Sulpice (left), which after Notre-Dame is the largest church in Paris, and St-Etienne-du-Mont (right), a singular church in which the Gothic styling shows signs of the innovative new wind of the Renaissance.*

44 top
During the time of Louis XVIII, portrayed here in his sumptuous coronation gowns (left), and during a party given in his honor at the Odéon Theater in 1819 (right), no one was concerned with changing or enriching the face of Paris.

44–45 *At the behest of Napoléon and in honor of the victory of the Grande Armée, a column based on Trajan's column in Rome was erected in the Place Vendôme. Cast from the bronze of melted cannons taken from the enemies at Austerlitz, the column is a continuous spiral of historical bas-reliefs.*

45 top left *Like his predecessor Louis XVIII, Charles X did little in the way of providing Paris with new architectural works.*

45 top right *The construction of the Arc de Triomphe, begun by Napoléon Bonaparte in 1806, was completed during the reign of Charles X.*

45 bottom right *On October 25, 1836, a great obelisk from Luxor was erected in the Place de la Concorde.*

The revolution's only great monument was the patriotic expanse of the Champs-de-Mars parade ground, the stage for national celebrations and military exercises. After the sober, precious Louis XVI style and the neoclassicism of the Directory, with its richer architectural features, the glory of Napoléon Bonaparte was celebrated in the first decades of the 19th century in monumental works. The marble Arc de Triomphe was erected at the end of the Champs-Élysées, the Rue de Rivoli was relaid, and at the center of the Place Vendôme a column cast in bronze from enemy cannons captured at Austerlitz was inaugurated on August 15, 1810. A symbol of the glorious Napoleonic era, it was decorated with a bas-reliefs depicting the feats of the Grande Armée.

The 19th century advanced with political instability under the new rulers Louis XVIII (1815–1824) and his successor, Charles X. The Romantics, with their long hair, red vests, and flowing shirts, challenged the conservatives with the dreams of liberty brought forth in their work. The heroic symbol of this period was *Hernani*, by Victor Hugo, which opened one memorable evening on the stage of the Théâtre Français.

46 top and 46–47
Baron Haussmann, receiving from Napoléon III the decree annexing the suburban communes to Paris, was responsible for the conception of the 19th-century city. Gutting and levelling whole quarters, building others from scratch, laying out broad streets to meet the new demands of urban traffic, within a few years Haussmann imposed upon medieval, baroque, and romantic Paris a modern, imperial vision of the capital, the plan of which can be seen reproduced above.

47 top
This painting embellished with pretty cherubs depicts the monumental Louvre complex at the time of Napoléon III. The emperor is portrayed in the frieze at the top.

47 bottom and center
The demolition of Paris by Haussmann provoked great controversy. In 1859, the poet Charles Baudelaire wrote, "The old Paris is no more." Two buildings erected during this period were the Opéra Garnier (top), considered a model of the Baroque style that characterized the reign of Napoléon III, and Les Halles (bottom), the central market, built between 1852 and 1859.

In February 1848, the Second Republic was proclaimed (the first had a short life during the revolution of 1792), with the unanimous election of Louis Napoléon Bonaparte as its leader. Four years later, he would assume the title of emperor of the French and the name Napoléon III. The Second Empire, which concluded in 1870, was a period of relative liberalism: The field of art saw the explosion of Impressionism; literature flourished with works of protest and rebellion; and Paris itself was subjected to the daring urban transformations of Baron Georges Haussmann, who for 40 years forced Parisians to walk through the mud of construction sites that were to provide the city with the most beautiful streets in the world.

The city suffered serious damage during the Franco-Prussian War and in the subsequent months when the French regular army besieged the capital in a cruel attempt to put down the insurrection that broke out after the surrender.

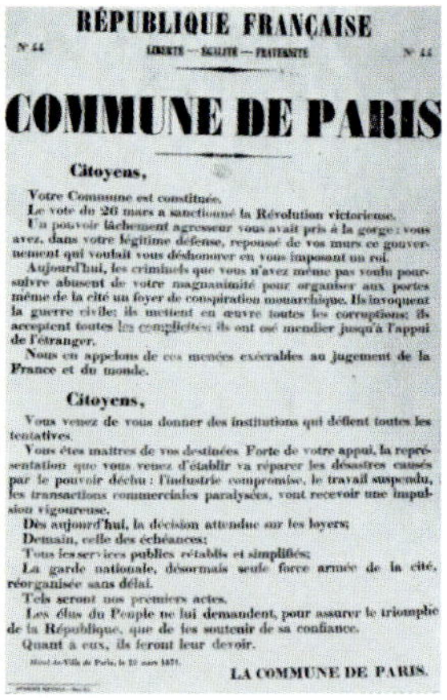

RÉPUBLIQUE FRANÇAISE

N° 44 LIBERTÉ — ÉGALITÉ — FRATERNITÉ N° 44

COMMUNE DE PARIS

Citoyens,

Votre Commune est constituée.

Le vote du 26 mars a sanctionné la Révolution victorieuse.

Un pouvoir lâchement agresseur vous avait pris à la gorge : vous avez, dans votre légitime défense, repoussé de vos murs ce gouvernement qui voulait vous déshonorer en vous imposant un roi.

Aujourd'hui, les criminels que vous n'avez même pas voulu poursuivre abusent de votre magnanimité pour organiser aux portes même de la cité un foyer de conspiration monarchique. Ils invoquent la guerre civile; ils mettent en œuvre toutes les corruptions; ils acceptent toutes les complicités; ils ont osé mendier jusqu'à l'appui de l'étranger.

Nous en appelons de ces menées exécrables au jugement de la France et du monde.

Citoyens,

Vous venez de vous donner des institutions qui défient toutes les tentatives.

Vous êtes maîtres de vos destinées. Forte de votre appui, la représentation que vous venez d'établir va réparer les désastres causés par le pouvoir déchu : l'industrie compromise, le travail suspendu, les transactions commerciales paralysées, vont recevoir une impulsion vigoureuse.

Dès aujourd'hui, la décision attendue sur les loyers;

Demain, celle des échéances;

Tous les services publics rétablis et simplifiés;

La garde nationale, désormais seule force armée de la cité, réorganisée sans délai.

Tels seront nos premiers actes.

Les élus du Peuple ne lui demandent, pour assurer le triomphe de la République, que de les soutenir de sa confiance.

Quant à eux, ils feront leur devoir.

Hôtel-de-Ville de Paris, le 29 mars 1871.

LA COMMUNE DE PARIS.

48 *With a series of state interventions, Napoléon attempted to meet the demands of a country in the process of transformation. During this period, roads, canals, and railway networks expanded and great avenues, squares, and sumptuous buildings were created. Napoléon III's policy was designed to revive the spirit of revolutionary France, but the war of 1870 consumed this euphoria and laid the basis for the fall of the imperial regime. The revolt exploded in Paris on March 18, 1871: the Commune was constituted as a revolutionary government. The illustrations on this page depict the salient events of those days: at the top, the revolutionaries and the manifesto of the Commune; in the center, the assembled representatives of the Commune; bottom, the disturbances in the capital.*

The Third Republic followed the violent struggles between the National Assembly (still controlled by the monarchy) and the revolutionary government, known as the Commune, which was installed in Paris on March 18, 1871. In a few short weeks, the new revolutionary regime demonstrated the validity of applied socialism, an event that later served as an exemplar for Karl Marx. The restoration of peace coincided with the birth of Impressionism, the art movement led by Monet, Renoir, Pissarro, Cézanne, and Manet. The first exhibition was held in the studio of the photographer Nadar, but it was not until 1877 that the term *Impressionistes* was officially acknowledged.

49 top and center
Two contemporary illustrations of the Prussians besieging and bombarding the capital at the end of the Franco-Prussian war.

49 bottom
After the fall of the Empire, the Third Republic was proclaimed. This contemporary print illustrates the general euphoria the event provoked.

50 top left and center left
The Belle Époque was a period of frenetic creativity: Art Nouveau—the work of A. Mucha (top left) was a synthesis of the airy canons of the style—and an evening at the Folies-Bergère (center left) were not to be missed.

50 center right
An unusual photograph of a moment in the construction of the Statue of Liberty. The statue was presented to the United States by France.

At the end of the century, Paris blossomed in the fields of art, music, and the theater. The city became the stage for the birth of modernity: The Belle Époque dawned, Art Nouveau burst onto the scene, the first Metro lines were laid, and gas lighting was adopted. The unmistakable outline of the Eiffel Tower climbed into the sky. In the first decade of the new century, Braque and Picasso overturned old artistic canons with Cubism, inaugurating an extraordinary period of creativity that fueled artists such as Fernand Léger and Marcel Duchamp. At the same time, Europe was heading toward one of the most tragic periods of its history.

50 bottom *A typical Paris Metro station. Work on the system began late in 1898 under the direction of Fulgence Bienvenue. The entrances were conceived in the style of the age, and 141 of them were designed by Hector Guimard, father of French Art Nouveau.*

50–51 *Scenes from the 1889 World's Fair in Paris: the main entrance (bottom), an exhibition hall (top right), and the fair's dominating symbol the Eiffel Tower (top left), designed by French engineer Alexandre-Gustave Eiffel. As it climbed into the capital's sky, the celebrated Iron Lady aroused fierce controversy, and its detractors signed petitions of disgust and condemnation of the bizarre construction. Many intellectuals entered the debate, claiming that the beauty of Paris would be ruined by that "ugly factory chimney."*

52 *These photographs illustrate some of the key moments in the recent history of Paris, in particular the occupying German army marching victoriously through the Arc de Triomphe (top). The photograph at bottom right portrays General de Gaulle against the backdrop of the Arc de Triomphe. The bottom left photograph depicts Parisian joy on the occasion of the Allies' entrance into Paris.*

During World War I the city was saved from an invasion of German troops, but during World War II, the German army marched beneath the Arc de Triomphe. The city folded in on itself. After the capitulation, General Charles de Gaulle launched an appeal from the studios of the BBC asking the French people to continue the resistance against the Germans. Finally, the Allies landed in Normandy, and Nazi Germany was defeated.

The Fourth Republic saw a series of unstable governments that hindered economic recovery. The war in Indochina concluded in defeat for France, and on the horizon loomed the dramatic prospect of war with Algeria. The Fifth Republic formed in 1958 after General de Gaulle was elected president. This relaunched France on the international scene. In 1962, de Gaulle signed the Evian Accords, which ended the war in Algeria.

53 top and center *Paris is not the city it was 100 years ago. Its center has been depopulated to make way for offices, banks, and international corporations, but the city's appeal endures intact, despite the devastating upheavals of May 1968.*

53 bottom
The last three presidents of France did their utmost for the city. On the left is the investiture of President Pompidou, in the center Valéry Giscard d'Estaing, and, on the right, Mitterrand at the inauguration of the Louvre pyramid, accompanied by the architect I. M. Pei.

In May 1968, the protests of students and workers echoed through barricaded squares, signalling a significant moment in the city's history. Once order was restored, a number of concessions were made, including a reform of the education system. In the presidential elections of 1969, de Gaulle was defeated by Georges Pompidou, who was in turn succeeded by Valéry Giscard d'Estaing in 1974, and François Mitterrand in 1981. Leader of the socialist party, Mitterrand was reelected for a second term, but was then defeated by Jacques Chirac in the elections of 1995.

These last presidents were the moving spirits behind new developments in Paris. Pompidou bequeathed his name to the bizarre Beaubourg, called "the blue refinery" by its detractors. Giscard d'Estaing approved the plans for the Musée d'Orsay, the Cité des Sciences et des Tecniques at La Villette, and the Institut du Monde Arabe. But the most ambitious projects were undertaken by François Mitterrand: the Grand Louvre; the Arche de la Défense; the Opéra-Bastille; and the Grande Bibliotèque, built "to preserve the historical memory of France" and, above all, to surprise the world and celebrate once again the eternal grandeur of Paris.

54 top and 55 top *The Ile de la Cité is the cradle of ancient Lutetia, the historic heart of the city. The island contains not only remains of the Roman* oppidum *and some of the city's most important monuments, such as Notre-Dame and Sainte-Chapelle, but also two of the most romantic and exclusive corners: the Square Galant and the intimate Place Dauphine, constructed at the behest of Henry IV to the design approved by Sully, in honor of the dauphin of France, the future Louis XIII.*

54–55 *The Seine and the Eiffel Tower are two symbols of the Ville Lumière. Despite being described as an old factory chimney by its detractors, the celebrated tower is one of the capital's most popular monuments. Work began on the tower in January 1887 and was completed two years later, just in time for the inauguration of the 1889 World's Fair.*

AN OPEN-AIR MUSEUM

Paris was born on two small islands in the Seine that are a world apart from the rest of the city and contain some of the capital's most significant monuments. The Ile de la Cité houses the roots of Gallic Lutetia, a village founded by a group of fisherman from the Parisii tribe in 200 BC, and seems to be frozen in the Grand Siècle, a era of elegant houses and silent streets, an oasis of peace and austere aristocracy. The Pont-Neuf, the oldest bridge in Paris, commissioned by Henry III in the late 16th century and opened by Henry IV in 1607 (a 19th-century statue depicting him mounted on his horse separates the tip of the island from the Place Dauphine) crosses into the living political and religious history of Paris.

55 right
Although the Ile St-Louis is linked to the Ile de la Cité, it is a world apart, isolated and deaf to the noise and bustle that surround it. Because of this exclusivity, the island has always housed celebrities, including Georges Pompidou, who had a home on Quai de Béthune, Baron Guy de Rothschild, and actress Michèle Morgan. In the 14th century, the island was a pasture for livestock. In the 17th century, the land was reclaimed and divided into lots. The streets that now crisscross the island are lined with beautiful 17-century buildings, a number of exclusive boutiques, and small bistros.

56 top left
The southern facade of the Palais de Justice faces the Quai des Orfèvres, where in the 12th and 13th centuries crafts workshops and jewelers flourished. This photograph shows the main entrance to the Palais de Justice, separated from the street by an imposing Louis XVI–style 18th-century gate.

56 bottom left
In the Conciergerie, the state prison during the Reign of Terror, are the Salle des Pas-Perdus and the Chambre Dorée, where in 1793 the sittings of the Revolutionary Tribunal led to the summary trials that sent guilty and innocent victims alike to the guillotine.

56 top right
Celebrated writer Georges Simenon identified the Palais de Justice with the imaginary "PJ," the legendary French judicial police of the detective Maigret.

56–57 and 57 top
Sainte-Chapelle, a jewel of Gothic art, has an airy, soaring structure and multicolored windows.

The Palais de Justice has the city's oldest public clock, one that has struck the hours for six centuries and was designed by German watchmaker Henri Vic in 1370. This building was the seat of the Paris Parliament when Charles V shifted the royal residence to the Louvre and became the Palais de Justice during the French Revolution. The stark walls of the Conciergerie and the adjoining sinister prison still evoke the tragic moments when those condemned to death during the Terror left from here, in white shirts, to be guillotined in the Place de la Concorde.

The precious Sainte-Chapelle, enclosed within the walls of the Palais de Justice, is a masterpiece of Gothic art. The chapel was built at the beginning of the 13th century at the behest of the sainted Louis IX, king of France, to house priceless relics of the Crown of Thorns and the Holy Cross from Byzantium. Its large stained-glass windows, which leave almost no room for the stonework, are a triumph of bright red and blue, and narrate scenes from Genesis, the Old Testament, and the life of Christ.

G.TRUFFAUT

58 *The beautiful west facade of the cathedral of Notre-Dame with the three-part vertical structure accentuated by the portals. Restoration work on Notre-Dame was begun in 1845 and completed in 1864 by architect Eugène Emmanuel Viollet-le-Duc.*

The most precious monument of the Ile de la Cité is the Cathedral of Notre-Dame, towering and immense on the Place du Parvis-Notre-Dame, a clearing created by Haussmann at the time of Napoléon III to display the building's celebrated facade and that conceals the vestiges of the primitive Gallic Lutetia. "Every wall, every stone of this venerable monument is a page not only from the history of France," wrote Victor Hugo, "but also of science and art. Among all the old churches of Paris, this central, mother-church is a kind of chimera: it has the head of this, the limbs of that, and the torso of another, something from everything. Each flux of time has brought its own alluvial deposit, every race has made its own contribution to the monument, each individual has added a stone. Like great mountains, great buildings are also the works of centuries."

In 1163, during the reign of Louis VII, Bishop Maurice de Sully invited Pope Alexander III to lay the foundation stone of the cathedral. On the foundations of an earlier Church of St. Stephen, a new basilica was erected. The construction of Notre-Dame took almost 200 years and was finished midway through the 14th century. Almost every event in the history of France has had an effect on the cathedral, including the French Revolution, which "consecrated" the cathedral to the cult of the God of Reason, plundering and sullying it in the process. A walk around the outside of Notre-Dame reveals the masterful interplay of architectural elements: rampant arches, spires, peaks, windows, doors, rose windows, and a magical population of monsters and demons emerging from magnificent doorways or springing out from pilasters garlanded with acanthus.

The view from the top of Notre-Dame's towers is a panorama of Paris and the nearby Ile St-Louis. Linked to the Ile de la Cité by the Pont St-Louis, this island is quiet and relatively undisturbed by tourism, a tongue of land laid gently down in the Seine and the residence of many of the capital's leading figures. This island has a succession of 17th-century patrician residences, including the Hôtel de Lauzun, which housed the poet Charles Baudelaire and members of the bohemian artistic and literary circles of his time.

59 top left
The Gallery of the Kings, only part of which can be seen here, contains 19th-century copies of 28 statues of the French kings. The originals were destroyed during the Revolution.

59 bottom left
In front of the western rose-window are the Virgin Mary and, to either side, representations of the virtues and vices.

59 right
The entrances of Notre-Dame are heavily decorated with fine sculptures. In these photographs are two details of the Door of the Virgin, the sculptures for which were executed in the 13th century.

60–61 *Gothic architecture flourished in France between the 11th and the 15th centuries and can be seen in many cathedrals from the era. Among the most famous of these is undoubtedly the Cathedral of Notre-Dame, the most venerated Parisian church, begun in 1163 at the behest of Louis VII and completed over the next 200 years. The cathedral was intended to rival the nearby St-Denis and earned literary immortality in the famous novel by Victor Hugo as the setting for the unhappy stories of Esmeralda and Quasimodo.*

A number of significant chapters in the history of France have been written in the building: Here Mary Stuart was married; Joan of Arc was proclaimed a saint; Abelard met Heloïse; Henry VI of England was crowned as the child king of France; Napoléon crowned himself emperor of the French in 1804; and in 1944, General de Gaulle announced the end of the German occupation of Paris. During the French Revolution,the cathedral was stripped of its treasures. In the autumn of 1793, vandals destroyed many of the statues, and the building was consecrated to the God of Reason. Notre-Dame was reconsigned to the Church in 1795, purified, and in 1802 once again held Catholic services. A small door near the north tower leads to the top of the cathedral and a stunning panoramic view of the city.

64 *Historic figures such as Diderot, Baudelaire, and Alfred de Musset have strolled along the avenues of the Luxembourg Gardens. De Musset defined the gardens as "a delightful place, a solitary haven open day and night for the student with his books under his arm, for the dreamer and his indolence and for the lover with his beloved who meet here as if in Paradise."*

The Luxembourg Gardens encircle the Palais du Luxembourg (today occupied by the senate of the Republic of France), the Florentine island constructed to remind Maria de' Medici of the Palazzo Pitti in Florence. At all hours of the day students linger on the terraces of the bars or in the windows of the bistros in the Latin Quarter, so named because in medieval times the official language used by professors and students was Latin and because this community—bounded by the Luxembourg Gardens, the Seine, and the Boulevard St-Michel—is built upon the ancient plan of the Gallic Lutetia. Not far from here, Caesar's shadow is still cast on the Arènes de Lutèce, an amphitheater constructed in the heart of ancient Lutetia (c. 1st century AD) and unearthed in 1869 during an excavation of the Rue Monge, and on the Cluny Baths, where, amid green fields and thick forests, the Romans relaxed.

The Musée National du Moyen-Age and the Cluny Baths contain the remains of three large rooms: the *frigidarium*, the *tepidarium*, and the *calidarium*. Backing onto the baths and built late in the 15th century is the Hôtel des Abbés de Cluny, itself the custodian of a collection of rare masterpieces of medieval art, including the six tapestries based upon the theme of the "Dame à la licorne," masterpieces of Flemish textile art.

64–65 *The Luxembourg Gardens officially belong to the Senate and surround the grandiose building of the same name in which the senators assemble. The gardens are the refuge of the students from the nearby universities and people searching for peace and tranquility.*

65 top *The Luxembourg Gardens were created in 1617 by Boyeau de la Bareaudière, the first authority on French-style gardens. The majority of the numerous statues set along the avenues were erected during the reign of Louis-Philippe, in the 19th century.*

The Left Bank is also rich in famous churches: St-Severin in the Flemish Gothic style, described by Huysmans as "delicate and small in a poor corner of Paris," where it's said that Dante came to pray during his supposed trip to Paris; St-Julien-le-Pauvre, in the heart of the university life of the city, encircled by the tight alleys (and near the church, at Place Viviani, grows the oldest tree in Paris, a false acacia or *Robinia*, planted in 1601 by botanist J. Robin, from whom the species takes its name); and St-Etienne-du-Mont, just a stone's throw from the Panthéon, noted for the decoration of its splendid Renaissance *jubé* as well as for the remains of St. Geneviève, the patron saint of Paris, buried in a chapel not far from Pascale and Racine. Finally, there is the most famous church in Paris and also the oldest: St-Germain-des-Prés, the abbey founded in 543 by King Childebert in the open countryside, on the vast plain where the Parisii were defeated by the Roman legionnaires. The interior has three naves, beautiful capitals on the choir stalls, and frescoed walls; up high, the sharp spires of a Romanesque bell tower preside over one of the liveliest squares on the Left Bank, not far from St-Sulpice, the largest church in Paris after Notre-Dame.

At the end of the Boulevard St-Germain, along the Quai St-Bernard, sparkles the curved facade of the Institute du Monde Arabe, built in 1987 by architect Jean Nouvel. The building is 10 stories high and has aluminium diaphragms, inspired by the Alhambra of Granada, that open and close according to the light of the sun, in a continuous dialogue between Arab architecture and modern technology. Beyond this is an oasis of peace: the Jardin des Plantes, the grandiose botanical gardens that surround the Musée National d'Histoire Naturelle. This was a royal garden of medicinal herbs during the reign of Louis XIII and was opened to the public in 1640. Mitterand commissioned a restoration of the building, which complements the metalwork of the Galerie de l'Évolution. The updated garden maintaims the exciting view of the long rows of stuffed giraffes, rhinoceroses, hippopotamuses, zebras, antelope, and elephants. From St-Germain-des-Prés, the Rue de Rennes meets Montparnasse and its most striking symbol: the Tour Montparnasse, a giant steel and glass structure that has been piercing the sky since 1973. The 688-foot tower has 59 stories that are climbed in an instant in an incredibly fast elevator, and it commands a breathtaking view of Paris.

It seems almost impossible to tie together the threads of this small hill's past, the myths woven around it by Apollinaire and the artists who at the beginning of the 20th century elected the area the "navel of the world," and the current urban agglomeration and the swarming of the populace at its feet. There remains the Musée Bourdelle on the Rue Antoine-Bourdelle to evoke something of the spirit that animated Montparnasse at the beginning of the 20th century. The studio of the celebrated sculptor (and favorite pupil of Rodin) houses more than 500 works of art that were created within its walls between 1884 and 1929, the year of the artist's death.

66–67 *In the twilight, Paris is illuminated like a fantastic stage set. Out of the shadows emerge the most distinguished monuments, cars trace bands of light along the grand boulevards (Rue de Rennes is outlined on the left), and the city unfurls its joie de vivre in anticipation of the adventures of the night to come. This photograph shows the floodlit facades of the most celebrated churches of the Rive Gauche: St-Germain-des-Prés on the left and St-Sulpice on the right.*

69–69 *Against the backdrop of the stunning panorama from the top of the Eiffel Tower stands the imposing Tour Montparnasse, a steel and concrete building constructed in 1973.*

70 *A turn-of-the-century railway station, the Gare d'Orsay was designed by Victor Laloux. After a complete restoration, the building now houses one of the most prestigious and popular Parisian museums. This photograph shows the broad glazed vaults where steam trains once belched smoke and where today visitors admire some of the most famous works by artists from the period between 1848 and World War I.*

71 top left
The Card Players, *by Paul Cézanne, was painted between 1890 and 1895. Many art historians believe the angular treatment of the figures, particularly the player on the left, and of the table, anticipates Cubism.*

71 bottom left
Déjeuner Sur l'Herbe, by *Eduoard Manet, was executed in 1863 and was subsequently presented at the Salon des Refusés during the reign of Napoléon III.*

71 top right
Claude Monet's The Woman with the Umbrella.

71 bottom right
Pierre-Auguste Renoir was a prominent figure in the cultural and worldly fervor that characterized Paris in the late 19th century. He painted the Portrait of Margo *in 1878.*

The historic Gare d'Orsay, the 19th-century railway station on the left bank of the Seine in front of the Louvre, houses one of Paris's most prestigious museums. The museum displays the works of major artists who were working between the middle of the 19th century and the beginning of World War I. Erected in 1871 to connect the capital to Nantes, Toulouse, and Bordeaux, this railway station was later condemned to demolition. It was spared because of the clamor aroused by the absurd demolition of Les Halles and handed over to the winners of a competition to find the best project for its revival. This huge building, made of iron and stone from Buxi, was converted into the Musée d'Orsay by the Italian architect Gae Aulenti in 1986 and is now one of the largest and most visited museums of the capital. The immense central nave, where the steam locomotives used to belch smoke, has been transformed into a labyrinth of clear light and suspended walls, which leave visitors free to wander, rather than imposing a particular path. The museum has assembled the works of many 19th-century artists: Ingres and Delacroix; the acclaimed Impressionists once housed in the old Jeu de Paume Museum: Degas, Monet, Manet, Pissarro, Renoir, Cézanne, van Gogh, Gauguin, Seurat, Toulouse-Lautrec, and Matisse; the realists Daumier, Millet, Corot, and Courbet; academy painters; the furniture of Gallé; and the works of Camille Claudel.

73 top
Camille Pissarro, 1830–1903, captured the mysterious atmosphere of Paris in La Seine et le Louvre.

73 center left
La Chambre de Van Gogh en Arles, *by van Gogh, reveals the artists's strength and bold handling of paint.*

73 center right
Paul Gauguin, 1848–1903, was initially an Impressionist painter, but subsequently developed a very personal painting style. He painted Joyeusetés *in 1892.*

73 bottom left
Edgar Degas captured the grace and lightness of a group of classical ballerinas waiting to perform in his Danseuses Bleues *of 1893.*

73 bottom right
Henri de Toulouse-Lautrec immortalized La Clowness Cha-u-Kao du Moulin Rouge *in 1895.*

72 *After Napoléon III came to power in 1852 there was an ensuing explosion of creativity in all fields of life and the arts. Poets flourished and painters began to pay a greater attention to reality, giving rise to the successful periods of Realism and Impressionism. Other celebrated works conserved in the Musée d'Orsay were created during these fertile years, including this work by van Gogh depicting* L'Église d'Auverse-sur-Oise, *executed in 1890.*

74 top and 74–75 *Napoleonic monumental Paris is represented by the École Militaire (top right) and the broad expanse of the Champs-de-Mars, across which echo memories of the Grande Armée. Below the imposing gilded cupola of the Dôme (bottom) lie the remains of Napoléon Bonaparte in a sarcophagus (top left).*

Monumental Paris is dominated by the golden cupola of the Dôme, under which Napoléon Bonaparte rests. In this Paris of grand spaces, long views, and the sumptuous noble and bourgeois mansions of the nobility, the city celebrates its eternal grandeur. From the Champs-de-Mars to the École Militaire, the country's foremost military academy, military memories echo across the broad parade ground that could at one time accommodate 10,000 mounted troops and pervade the still atmosphere of the Musée de l'Armée, which displays hand-embroidered banners of various coats of arms and rich collections of weapons of all eras: swords, pistols, firearms, crossbows, muskets, armour, maps and plans, and flags. The Hôtel des Invalides, commissioned by Louis XIV to house injured, ill, or elderly retired soldiers, has a golden dome containing the porphyry tomb of Napoléon, according to his last wishes: "I would like my ashes laid to rest on the banks of the Seine, in the midst of the people of France, whom I have loved so much." A few steps away from the Dôme is the Musée Rodin, dedicated to artist who between the 19th and the 20th centuries filled the world with his celebrated sculptures, the eclectic romantic who opened the door to modernity for his contemporaries. At the beginning of the century, on the advice of his friend Rainer Maria Rilke, he established his studio-museum in the Hôtel Biron, which now houses the artist's bronze monuments and famous works like the *La Main de Dieu* and the celebrated *Kiss*.

75 *Near Les Invalides, at the end of Rue de Varenne, is the Musée Rodin, housed in the beautiful rooms of the Hôtel Biron. The photographs show the entrance to the museum (top), a room dedicated to one of the sculptor's most famous works, the celebrated* Kiss *(center), and Rodin's works exhibited in the garden, with the grandiose backdrop of the gilded dome over Napoléon's tomb (bottom).*

It took 7,300 tons of iron to build the Eiffel Tower, which, at the time it was built, was described as a "ridiculous factory fireplace" and "the gigantic skewer, good for poking the clouds." On June 12, 1886, engineer Alexandre-Gustave Eiffel won the city of Paris's competition when the World's Fair of 1889 chose his "grande dame of iron" as its symbol from among 107 proposals. The workers began construction at the beginning of January 1887, and soon all heads were turning upward to stare at the marvel of the century—such a strange construction that day by day climbed higher toward the sky. The official inauguration was held in May 1889. Since then, 6 million visitors a year have climbed to the top to take in the breathtaking view of Paris. At the tower's feet, the Pont d'Iéna crosses over the Seine and arrives at the hill of Chaillot, high against the right bank of the river and home to the semicircular Palais de Chaillot, constructed for the 1937 Paris exhibition. The building contains the Musée de la Marine, which takes visitors to the high seas; the Musée de l'Homme, a historical museum; and the Musée du Cinema Henri Langlois, Rudolph Valentino, Marilyn Monroe, Greta Garbo, and Federico Fellini are brought back to life.

76–77 *From the outset, the Eiffel Tower could be seen from all four corners of Paris. Today, the bizarre construction is no longer regarded with irony, but rather as the most acrobatic and glorious symbol of the city. It took two years to build the tower, which is 984 feet tall and is topped by an antenna that brings it to 1,043 feet. The 18,030 wrought-iron sections and 2.5 million rivets weigh a total of 10,000 tons. Climbing to the top on foot means walking up 1,665 steps.*

78 *The imposing Champs-Élyseés is lined with beautiful buildings.*

78–79 *The Arc de Triomphe is the hub around which are set the 8th, 16th, and 17th arrondissements. The Étoile is ringed by 12 architecturally symmetrical buildings that lend a sense of harmony to the monumental space.*

79 top left *Innumerable shops, bistros, and cafés face the Champs-Élyseés, and beneath the trees that line the boulevard is the continuous bustle of Parisian life.*

79 top right *In the center of the Rond Point stands the Arc de Triomphe, from which a number of the city's grandest boulevards radiate, as can be seen in this photo of the Étoile.*

Great flights of steps run down the sides of the hill, and intrepid youths execute skateboard stunts in the square. This is still the Paris of grand spaces and long views that lead to the Étoile and to the Arc de Triomphe, a solemn anthem to glorious victory. Upon his return from the Battle of Austerlitz in 1806, Napoléon commissioned this immense monument to celebrate his men's triumphant military campaign. The view in one direction from the top of the arch takes in the major artery that leads to the Grande Arche de la Défense, Otto von Spreckelsen's cube covered in white Carrara marble and inaugurated in the bicentennial of the French Revolution. In the other direction, the Champs-Élyseés leads to the Place de la Concorde and Les Tuileries. A military parade marches down this street every July 14, with much fanfare and fluttering of tricolor flags.

The old Vie Royale initially extended only to the Étoile, to extend the Tuileries gardens and to create a larger area for the king's pleasure. In the 18th century, the area was simply a walk through pastures and fields; in the first years of the 19th century, it already hosted a few buildings; and by the Second Empire, it featured great hotels and luxurious estates. Today, boutiques, cafés, movie theaters, airline offices, and the celebrated Lido are among the attractions of the most famous street in the world. The Champs-Élysées stretches to the Louvre. On the right of the Seine are the Pont Alexandre III and the scenic view of the Petit Palais and the Grand Palais. The latter are testimony to the era in which Paris, capital of science and technology, gathered together the nations of the world every 10 years to celebrate the marriage of Progress and Reason.

HUITRES

19h28

80 top *A number of views of the futuristic Quartier de la Défense, also known as "Wall Street-sur-Seine" because of the area's financial importance in recent years.*

80–81 *La Grande Arche de la Défense in the western suburbs of the city. The gigantic cube of white Carrara marble, more than 300 feet tall, could comfortably contain the entire Cathedral of Notre-Dame.*

81 *A symbol of challenge and modernity, La Grande Arche de la Défense, the work of Danish architect Von Spreckelsen, was backed by President Mitterrand as the home of the International Foundation for Human Rights and as a monumental work commemorating the bicentennial of the French Revolution.*

82–83 *Stone lions, allegorical statues, and grandiose lampposts, copies of those on the Trinity Bridge in St. Petersburg, lend a magical beauty to the Pont Alexandre III, which links the Esplanade des Invalides with the Champs-Élyseés. The bridge was named after Russian tsar Alexander III to mark the 1893 alliance between France and Russia and has a single span about 300 feet long.*

Enlarged and partially reorganized at the behest of Mitterrand, the Louvre houses the largest collection of art in the world. To fully appreciate the Louvre requires time and more tha one visit. The museum has so many highlights: the statues of the Cour Marly in the Richelieu Wing; the winged bulls of Korsabad; the *Venus de Milo*; *Winged Victory of Samothrace*; works by Michelangelo, Raphael, and Leonardo; 16th-century Dutch still-lifes; bucolic landscapes of Poussin and Watteau; and a seemingly endless sequence of masterpieces.

The musuem's entrance on the Rue de Rivoli is a remarkable sight. Architect I. M. Pei's inverted glass pyramid draws light from the larger, external pyramid that serves as the principle entrance to the Louvre at the center of the Cour Napoléon. Seen from below, the magical play of light and glass reflects the clouds and the silhouettes of tourists who seem to be suspended in midair, while the Parisian sky penetrates the hazy transparency of the glass, and sheds its silvery light upon the inverted pyramid below.

84–85 *The Louvre, in an aerial view, throws a new light on immortal masterpieces such as the* Winged Victory of Samothrace, *top right, and the* Venus de Milo, *bottom left.*

86 *The entrance to the Louvre is located below the glass pyramid designed by architect I.M. Pei and built in the center of the Cour Napoléon. The museum can also be reached via Rue de Rivoli via the Carrousel du Louvre.*

87 *The spacious, well-lit halls of the Louvre contain masterpieces from all eras and from all over the world. The world's greatest museum houses works of art dating back as far as 5,000 years BC as well as contemporary pieces.*

89 *Jan Vermeer's* The Lace-maker, *Raphael's portrait of Baldassare Castiglione; Eugène Delacroix's* Liberty Leading the People; *and Camille Corot's* Dame en Bleu *hang in the Louvre.*

88 *Among the innumerable masterpieces in the Louvre, the sweetly enigmatic smile of Leonardo da Vinci's* Mona Lisa *stands out.*

90 top
On one side of the Place de la Concorde, toward the Tuileries and the Louvre, stands the Arc de Triomphe du Carrousel, built at Napoléon's behest in 1806 and topped at that time by a copy of the celebrated horses from the Basilica of San Marco in Venice.

90–91 Place de la Concorde bears a name of peace despite the fact that, over the centuries, it has hosted public celebrations of the Ancien Régime, military charges, massacres, funeral processions, and last, but by no means least, the infamous guillotine that during the Reign of Terror fell on guilty and innocent necks alike. In the middle of the square rises the solemn obelisk from the Temple of Luxor.

At the end of the Cour Napoléon, the Arc de Triomphe du Carrousel, with its eight columns of pink marble, frames a celebrated view of the Champs-Élyseés. Bucolic in the shade in the Tuileries Gardens, yet regal in the vast arena of the Place de la Concorde, this is the setting for well-known celebrations, funeral processions, and military parades. The obelisk, from the Temple of Luxor, was placed in the middle of this square in the autumn of 1836, at the site where, from 1793 to 1795, the guillotine brought thousands of people, including Marie-Antoinette, to meet their maker. Kings and queens also haunt the nearby Church of St-Germain l'Auxerrois in the Place du Louvre. The church was once the parish church of the French sovereigns and was patronized by Francis I, Henry IV, and Louis XIV and dedicated to St-Germain, bishop of Auxerre.

91 *Place de la Concorde was enhanced in 1836 by architect Hittorff, who built the majestic fountains alongside the obelisk from the Temple of Luxor.*

92–93 *The Centre Pompidou rises in the heart of the city. The building's brightly colored tubes, exposed steel tie-rods, and external escalator enclosed in a transparent Plexiglas tube have been a source of controversy ever since the museum was built. It has nevertheless become the city's most popular cultural attraction.*

92 top
The futuristic Centre Pompidou faces the singular Igor-Stravinsky Plaza, which is characterized by the multicolored animated fountain designed by Niki de Saint-Phalle and Jean Tinguely.

92 bottom
The broad open space alongside the Beauborg provides a stage for numerous street artists who perform for hurrying Parisians and fascinated tourists.

The Musée des Arts Decoratifs and the Musée des Arts de la Mode offer a trip through time, with rooms packed with antique furnishings: Louis XV furniture, tapestries, jewels, fabrics, ceramics, glass, toys, rugs, objects from daily life, lace, and sumptuous clothing belonging to famous figures of the past.

Nearby, in the Jardin des Tuileries, the Musée de l'Orangerie displays Claude Monet's *Waterlilies*, Cézanne's still-lifes, Renoir's *Les Fillettes au Piano*, a number of *Odalisques* by Matisse, and, between a Picasso and a Modigliani, the Parisian scenes of Utrillo.

The strangest and most controversial, modern, and daring museum in Paris comes into sight suddenly at the corner of the Rue Rambuteau. The Centre Pompidou, the famous Beaubourg, is outfitted with improbable colored and transparent pipes and steel rods. This building is the creation of architects Renzo Piano, Gianfranco Franchini, and Richard Rogers, and it has frequently been likened to a colored refinery, a "modern idol of leaded Plexiglas, like a space station in the heart of the city." Visited annually by 7 million people, the Beaubourg is an ultramodern cultural center that includes a huge library of texts on figurative art and the Musée National d'Art Moderne.

93 top
"A unique original effort to unite and render accessible the various elements of modern culture in a single complex." This was the principal aim behind the most talked about and unusual of Paris's museums, inaugurated in 1977 and seen here in a stunning aerial photograph.

94–95 *The Centre National d'Art et de Culture Georges-Pompidou, better known as the Pompidou Centre or the Beauborg, contains the Museum of Modern Art. In this second museum are works by the greatest artists of the century, almost all of them masterpieces that once hung in the Museum of Modern Art created in 1937 and the National Center for Contemporary Art, which was created in 1967. The collections are on the fourth floor of the Pompidou Center and include* The Muse, *by Pablo Picasso (large photo right);* Lolotte, *by Amedeo Modigliani (top right); Georges Braque's* Young Girl and Guitar *(top left); and Giorgio de Chirico's* Premonitory Portrait of Apollinaire *(bottom). Alongside the works of these artists are those of the Fauve painters, such as Pierre Bonnard and Henri Matisse; the Cubists, including Fernand Léger and Braque; and the major movements from World War I to the 1960s.*

96 top
After a long period of neglect the Marais has experienced explosive rejuvenation. It is now the most fashionable area of the capital, the quarter with the most museums, aristocratic buildings, and trendy boutiques. Some of the streets retain their original atmosphere, but in others, the old shops and commercial stores have given way to art galleries and the most sophisticated fashion houses. In this photograph are a number of the sumptuous buildings facing Place des Vosges.

96–97 *The grand facade of the Hôtel de Ville borders the Marais. This prestigious building is set off by a broad square, formerly known as Place de Grève, where unemployed laborers congregated. It was here that the Republic was proclaimed on September 4, 1870, and it was to this building that Charles de Gaulle came on August 25, 1944. The current Hôtel de Ville dates from the end of the 19th century; a fire destroyed the earlier building.*

97 top *Place des Vosges was inaugurated to celebrate the marriage of Louis XIII and Anne of Austria and is a perfect 17th-century architectural jewel.*

97 bottom *The Musée Carnavalet occupies two historic buildings: the Hôtel Carnavalet, built in 1545 to the design of Nicolas Dupuis, and the Hôtel le Peletier de St-Fargeau, a building dating from the 17th century. The museum contains numerous paintings, sculptures, and engravings that reconstruct, in chronological order, the history of Paris.*

Behind the Beaubourg stretches the Marais, the ancient marsh that at one time extended all the way from the Place de la Concorde to the Bastille. Today, the Marais is the most fashionable district of the city. For 600 years, from the Dark Ages to the 18th century, this quarter of Paris was filled with the houses of the aristocracy, sumptuous apartments, churches, and convents. Place des Vosges is the area's most representative and enchanting corner. This royal playground was created for Henry IV initially as a garden for the *noblesse d'épée* (the ancient and noble art of swordsmanship). It is surrounded by redbrick buildings with slate roofs that create an extraordinary symmetry and is overlooked by an equestrian statue of Louis XIII. The area also hosts the ghosts of famous people who lived here, including, at number 6, Victor Hugo, whose house is today a museum of the relics and memories of the great writer; and the Marquess of Sévignée, born at number 1, the Hôtel de Coulange.

In adjacent streets stand other mansions: the Hôtel de Sens, where Queen Margaret, the wife of Henry IV, lived; the Hôtel Salé, which since 1985 has been home to one of the most extensive collections of the works of Picasso; the Hôtel de Sully, where temporary exhibitions are held; and the Hôtel Carnavelet, which contains the museum dearest to Parisian hearts. Here, among salons, stairways, and sumptuous furnishings, are all records of French history, ranging from the Declaration of the Rights of Man to Voltaire's painting chair, from Proust's bedroom to Jean-Jacques Rousseau's inkpot, from the walking stick of Emile Zola to the original, antique keys to the Bastille.

98 top *The Opéra Garnier is the eclectic, neobaroque palace that best expresses the architectural canons of the era of Napoléon III. The friezes, columns, domes, and bronze and marble statues, and the marriage of the classical and baroque styles create an overwhelming effect, and the building has in the past been compared with an enormous, sophisticated cream cake.*

98–99 *Sumptuous homes and glittering shop windows face the octagonal Place Vendôme. The square was designed by Jules Hardouin-Mansart and was destined to house a statue of Louis XIV.*

99 top *The daring and eccentric structure of the Opéra-Bastille houses one of the world's most famous ballet companies. This building was inaugurated in 1989 and can accommodate 2,700 spectators.*

99 bottom left *A detail of the famous column that rises in Place Vendôme. The tower was erected at the behest of Napoléon Bonaparte as a tribute to the Grande Armée.*

99 bottom right *The gilded Genius of Liberty stands atop the July Column, a monument more than 160 feet tall in the center of the Place de la Bastille and dedicated to the victims of the revolution of 1830.*

In the Place de la Bastille are the July Column, erected in memory of the victims of the revolution of 1830, and the Opéra-Bastille, the great modern palace of concrete, marble, and wood; it is the creation of Carlo Ott, who subverted the ancient concept of the theater. "No longer horseshoe halls, no longer gilded candy bowls in which sound spins as if it were inside the body of a cello," wrote Alessandro Baricco, "but megahalls, enormous spaces, gigantic stages, thousands of seats, and multiple galleries."

The right bank at the Place de la Concorde has become the epitome of luxury and supreme elegance. Jewelry glitters in the shop windows of the Place Vendôme, the architectural jewel created by Jules Hardouin-Mansart for Louis XIV. At the end of Rue de la Paix are the ostentatious, neobaroque Opéra Garnier, from the period of the Second Empire, and the Rue du Faubourg-St-Honoré, which houses Paris's most exclusive shops. The unmistakable profile of the Sacré-Coeur is visible in the distance. At some point every visitor inevitably arrive here: This hill, with its long flight of steps overlooking the roofs of the city, is where the Paris of myths still lives.

In a tree-lined square, lined with artists ready to paint your portrait, with the brilliant whiteness of the Church of the Sacré-Coeur, the blazing lights of the Pigalle, and the worn walls of the Bonne Franquette, it is still possible to imagine those roaring years in which Montmartre brought forth its memorable contributions to art and the outbursts of those restless, aimless youths of the most legendary bohemia.

100 top and 100 top
Montmartre was the focus for a remarkable period in the history of the arts. An entire generation of artists contributed to the creation of its reputation: Degas, Cézanne, Delacroix, Monet, and Van Gogh all lived, suffered, and painted here. Today, few traces remain of their presence.

The early Bohème of Renoir and Lautrec was at the top or the foot of the hill, and 20 years later Picasso, Juan Gris, Van Dongen, and Modigliani arrived to make their contribution to the legend of the quarter. Today, the narrow streets swarm with mimes, hawkers, and buskers.

100 bottom
Numerous painters, especially in Place du Tertre, attempt to revive the distant memories of a Montmartre that is no more.

100–101
The majestic white Sacré-Coeur basilica dominates the hill of Montmartre and was the fruit of a vow made by two businessmen, Alexandre Legentil and Rohault de Fleury, at the beginning of the Franco-Prussian War of 1870. The brothers promised that if France was victorious in the bloody conflict, they would erect a church dedicated to the Sacred Heart of Christ. The work, under the direction of Guilbert, the city architect of the era, began in 1875, and the church was consecrated in 1919, after the victorious outcome of World War I.

102 center left *The Train Bleu is the restaurant at the Gare de Lyon, the station from which trains to the south depart. The station's great stuccoed halls are painted with 19th-century frescoes that depict the most famous tourist destinations on the Mediterranean Riviera.*

102 bottom left and right *The cafés of Paris are not mere refuges of conversation and relaxation; some of them, like the Deux-Magots, in the bottom right photograph, have contributed to the Parisian legend.*

Where to begin to share in the intimacy and spirit, emotions and charms, secrets and memories of this great capital of dreams? In the museums or during a walk along the Seine? In front of the latest, most controversial piece of architecture, or in a chic café on the Champs-Élysées? Among the crowds on the boulevards or beneath the trees of the lonely Vert Galant? Walking, walking, and more walking is the key to establishing an open dialogue with this city, which at every corner changes face and dimension, stirring memories and promising a surprise at every turn.

102 top left *The Café de Flore was a permanent home for Jean-Paul Sartre and Simone de Beauvoir during the era of the Existentialists.*

There are many facets to this city: history, shopping, art, the joys of life, wild nights, cozy bistros, merchants, intellectuals, glittering shop windows, the most improbable future, long boulevards, and modernity. Within the great well of the city's golden history, dreams, and fantasies, every visitor finds his or her own beloved, unforgettable Paris, that mythical Paris everyone yearns to experience. Along the banks of the Seine, the serene and lofty river of poets and artists that divides the city into two worlds, the *bouquinistes* of the Rive Gauche, the oldest tenants of the Pont-Neuf, have been selling books and pamphlets since the 17th century. At night they lock their goods into cases of green-painted wood, an ancient custom that continues to this day, and one reproduced on countless postcards. In the gloomy half-light of Notre-Dame, pierced only by a few irridescent rays breaking through the stained-glass windows, the ghosts of history may be perceived. Here Mary Stuart was married, Joan of Arc was proclaimed a saint, Abelard met the demure Heloïse, and Napoléon crowned himself emperor of France, wrapped in a pale brocade cloak

103 Along the Champs-Élysées are cafés that offer an opportunity to rest in the leafy shade of the trees lining the boulevard.

104 top left *The display windows of Cartier, the celebrated Parisian jeweler, overlook Rue de la Paix, the attractive street built for Napoléon in 1806, inaugurated in 1814, and named in commemoration of the peace treaty.*

104 bottom left
The Galeries Lafayette, near the Opéra, is one of the most famous Parisian department stores. It started out quietly as a small boutique at the corner of La Fayette and Chausée-d'Antin and was expanded early in the 20th century.

104 right
The interior of the Galeries Lafayette has balustrades attributed to Majorelle and an imposing glazed dome. Today, the great store is composed of three large interconnected buildings.

embroidered with tiny golden bees. Little shops and restaurants and Berthillon, the famous ice-cream shop that makes the best ice cream in Paris, enliven the nearby Rue St-Louis-en l'Ile, an intimate street far removed from the Paris of broad spaces and conspicuous modernity. St-Germain-des-Prés is just a step away, on the left bank of the Seine, and is home to the Flore and the Deux-Magots cafés and the brasserie Lipp. Here the ideas that stirred the hearts and souls of a generation were born. The powerful and rebellious atmosphere of the golden 1960s once thrived here. Jean-Paul Sartre and Simone de Beauvoir were permanent fixtures at the Café de Flore, and with them their existentialist followers, unshaven and dressed in black turtle-neck sweaters and duffel coats rather than bourgeois overcoats. In this neighborhood, Yves Montand and Juliette Gréco took their first steps in what later became glorious careers. Today, the most stylish shopping streets branch off from the axis of the Boulevard St-Germain-des-Prés; luxury flirts with bohemia on Rue du Bac, Rue de Grenelle, and Rue de Sèvres, and fashion triumphs.

A world of fine antiques can be found a few blocks away along the Quai Voltaire, the mythical *carré d'or*, with all the unspoiled appeal of old Paris; the area bounded by the Rue de l'Université and Rue des Sts-Pères is home to nearly 100 art shops.

Montparnasse is in full sail at the

105 *The* passages *and the* galeries *are covered alleys that link two or more of the streets in a particular quarter. They were a very fashionable architectural feature in the early 20th century, partly because gas lamps made them particularly attractive at night. These photographs show the Passage Verdeau, with its entrance at 6 Rue de la Grange-Batelière (top left), and the Galerie Vivienne, created in 1823.*

107 top left *Montmartre has lost the personalities responsible for creating the legend of the celebrated* butte *(hill), but as the poet Gérard de Nerval once wrote, little has changed, "there are still windmills, cabaret and greengrocers, rural paradises and silent alleys flanked by overgrown gardens." It was on this hill that St. Denis, the first bishop of Lutetia, was decapitated (hence the name* mons martyrum *transformed into Montmartre). In the 12th century, a Benedictine abbey, Dames de Montmartre, was built in the fields and vineyards. The building was razed during the revolution. In the top left is a tearoom sign.*

107 top right *Rue Lepic, a historic street in the legendary Montmartre district, where Vincent van Gogh once lived. At the end of the street are the sails of the Moulin du Radet, located not far from the more famous Moulin de la Galette.*

106 *Two tourists observing the facade of Au Lapin Agile, an unusually rustic nightspot built in 1910 and for many years the home of literary circles.*

106–107 *The still sails of Paris's most famous windmill, the Moulin Rouge, are today a destination for tourists in search of a taste of the wilder, more carefree side of Parisian life.*

end of Rue de Rennes, its bright, soaring mainmast represented by the vertiginous tower of glass and cement. This area bustles with life and at night cloaks itself in the red lights of the more risqué shows and the myriad lamps of the bistros (including the renowned Coupole and Dômme, the former favorites of Mirò, Picasso, Hemingway, and Chagall). But the world of energetic *filles de joie*, young models with painted flowers on their calves and watches saucily attached to their garters, is far away. Remote is the world of *Kiki of Montparnasse*, the quarter's symbol immortalized in the photographs of Man Ray. His nude portraits of her have found their way into museums all over the world.

At the beginning of the century Montparnasse took the place of Montmartre, another legendary temple of the bohemian Paris of 100 years ago, colored with love, avant-garde art, and contradictions. In 1887, Degas, Cézanne, Monet, and many other artists lived upon the hill dominated by the Sacré-Coeur basilica. They were all friends and met at the Place du Tertre and danced together at country fairs in front of the Moulin de la Galette. In the same era, at the window of his room on Rue Lepic, Vincent van Gogh painted the roofs of Montmartre. Today, Montmartre exists in flux between memory and consumerism, old quarters and new restaurants, false and authentic artists, the Moulin Rouge and Pigalle, and the heritage of those memories left upon the stubby hill—the *butte*, that has the Place de Tertre as its fulcrum—by a generation of legendary artists. Visitors climb upward, as if on a pilgrimage, to search for a world of memories, to gaze from above upon the grey roofs of Paris and the immobile sails of the Moulin Rouge, the mythical haunt of Montmartre's prime.

A trip to Paris is inconceivable without an excursion to its shops, boutiques, and famous stores. In the sumptuous lounge of Faubourg St-Honoré or in the windows of the *triangle d'or*, reigns the world of haute couture and the most prestigious fash-

CAFÉ
SALON DE THÉ

UN ROUGE
DU
MOULIN RO
FORMIDABLE
FORMIDABLE
FORMIDABLE
FORMIDABLE

108–109 *A trip by* bateau-mouche *is a classic for first-time visitors to Paris. Seen from the river, Paris offers broad panoramas that include the austere buildings reflected in the Seine, the Cathedral of Notre-Dame, and the bridges linking the left and right banks. From the Quai de Bercy, to the east, to Billancourt on the other side of the city, no less than 36 bridges cross the Seine. Not all of the constructions are as old as the Pont-Neuf, the first stone bridge to link the two sides of the capital, nor are they all as attractive as the Pont Alexandre III or as famous as the Pont Mirabeau, celebrated by the poet Guillaume Apollinaire.*

ion houses. On the élite Place Vendôme or Rue de la Paix, the window displays ooze luxury and elegance.

Behind the Opéra is the colorful bustle of the most famous department stores. These are located along the grandiose boulevards designed by Baron Haussmann under Napoléon III—a new, modern and imperial city built atop the flattened remains of the romantic and baroque medieval Paris.

The appeal of the old Marais, the city's Jewish quarter and today the most fashionable district in Paris, has been retained intact. The quarter is a maze of narrow streets and trendsetting boutiques grouped around the Place des Vosges, the most romantic and celebrated of the city's squares. Here are fascinating little museums devoted to the secret treasures of past lives: the Museum of Romantic Life; the Edith Piaf Museum, dedicated to the fragile and magnetic French *chanteuse*; and the Museum of Merry-Go-Rounds and Theater Design. There is also the alluring weekend market of St-Ouen, the largest flea market in the world.

But Paris would not be Paris if, at sunset, the lights of a romantic restaurant, the colorful buzz of a brasserie, the sequins and spangles of the irresistible Folies-Bergère, or the artful rite of the eternal can-can did not take center stage.

109 top
It was the Pont-Neuf, the jewel of town planning built at the behest of Henry IV, that housed the first book-sellers, the bouquinistes, *who still today represent one of the best-loved postcard images of Paris. Along the banks of the Seine, near the Pont-Neuf and the Cathedral of Notre-Dame, they display secondhand books and old prints and postcards. At night, the books are locked into green-painted wooden containers hung on the parapets along the river.*

110 top
The broad expanse of the Champ-de-Mars is all the more evocative at night, when skillful lighting emphasizes the great spaces and the solid structure of the École Militaire. On the left of the photograph is the gilded dome of the Hôtel des Invalides.

110 bottom
Paris, with its historic quarters clearly defined.

110–111
The Bastille, the center of a new revolution in a quarter with a wealth of crafts workshops, cafés, and bistros that have grown up around the controversial Opéra-Bastille. At the center of the square, where a 160-foot column now rises, once stood the famous fortress-prison of the Ancien Régime. The prison was stormed on July 14, 1789, at the very start of the French Revolution.

111 top *The unmistakable sign of the Paris Métro at Porte Dauphine, known as the Libellule, is a splendid example, the last remaining, of the creative genius of Hector Guimard, the father of French Art Nouveau, who early this century, designed these remarkable entrances for the underground railway system.*

112–113 *Paris, the romantic city par excellence, reveals all its appeal and mystery.*

VERSAILLES: GOLD LEAF, MIRRORS, AND ABSOLUTE POWER

114 top
The main building of the Palace of Versailles reflected in the central pool.

114 bottom
The Temple of Love, created for Marie Antoinette, is enclosed in the dense vegetation of the park of Versailles.

114–115
The architecture of the entire Versailles complex was intended to be an expression of regal opulence. The palace was built for Louis XIV, who fell in love with the design of architect Le Vau. When the palace was almost completed, the king transferred his court there from Paris. The king personally oversaw the work of the landscape gardener Le Nôtre, who was responsible for the design of the green areas such as the great lawn and the parterre to the north planted with flowers and box hedges.

Beyond a gilded gateway opens the door to an epoch marked by the glories of the French monarchy. The forest of mirrors, the immense staircases, the silk-lined salons, damask curtains, and gigantic crystal chandeliers witnessed processions of courtiers, princes, high prelates, and ambassadors come to pay homage to the Sun King. Far away, under the arch of the Salon de la Paix, the king sat solemnly on a throne 10 feet tall, set on a carpet of gold. The Marquess of Sévigné described the palace of Versailles as "a regal beauty unique in the world."

At every step Versailles reminds visitors of the infinite power wielded by Louis XIV and his successors. In 1623, the joy of hunting, of the woods, and fresh, fragrant air, and the satisfaction of an overflowing game bag led Louis XIII to build, in this place, a *pavillon de chasse*, later transformed into a larger edifice, the *petit château de cartes* of stone and brick, traces of which can still be seen in the facade of the Cour de Marbre, which remains almost completely intact to this day.

In 1661, Louis XIV, reluctant to demolish his father's favorite hunting lodge, decided to transform it into a much larger complex with the help of architect Le Vau. The work begun then was to last until the end of his reign. Initially, the king used the small castle as a refuge for his romantic dalliances with the beautiful Louise de la Vallière, and he created a fairy-tale park around the hunting lodge where he modeled nature after his dreams.

Versailles was transformed into a magnificent baroque palace, the king's finest achievement. In 1666, after the death of his mother, Anna of Austria, Louis XIV began to consider

115 top
Hundreds of statues are scattered throughout the immense park at Versailles. The particularly stunning gilded statues of Basin de Latona (left) and the Apollon (right) adorn the celebrated fountains in the great garden.

116 *Louis XIV was obsessed with the Palace of Versailles and dedicated himself to the building throughout his reign. The apartments and the great halls, such as the Salon de Diane (right) and the Opéra Royal (left), with the gallery decorated by Pajou, reflect the king's dedication to decorative splendor and opulence.*

Versailles more seriously as the principal residence for the sovereign and his court. In 1682, the king moved to this great complex, which became the most extraordinary *ville royale* in the world. Ten thousand courtiers (including 5,000 noblemen) were fed in the court dining rooms every day. They surrounded the king and served him with dignity and honor. In 1683, the king opened the doors of his apartments to his court, hosting dances, games, and spectacles for their amusement. If in 1661 the little village of Versailles was just a handful of houses in the country, by 1713 it was a town of 45,000 inhabitants. The *ville nouvelle*, as it was known at the time, was connected to Paris by an incessant coming and going of horses, carriages, and carts.

The immense estate that enclosed the palace was surrounded by a 25-mile-long wall that was broken with 24 monumental gates (of which only five remain today). Only a small part of the primitive park remains but the palace and the grounds are still magnificent.

Versailles preoccupied Louis XIV throughout his reign. He found the ideal interpreter and accomplice for his most fantastic projects in Le Nôtre, the celebrated architect of the gardens. Le Nôtre conceived for the king not a garden, but a baroque city, full of surprises. He modeled nature as though it were a theater, resorting to every type of visual trick, great screens of trees, and numerous little woods growing in every corner enclosing mythological statues, playful fountains, or unexpected labyrinths. He flooded the Grand Canal, upon which Venetian gondolas and a flotilla of miniature warships glided.

The court remained at Versailles until 1789, when the Revolution forced Louis XVI to return to Paris. In the face the rebellion, on the night of October 6 of that year, the king left the palace through a spectacular secret passage to rejoin his queen, Marie-Antoinette, who had already escaped by another route. Versailles was ransacked during the revolution and soon fell into ruins, as did the park and all its marvels.

In 1837, the Chamber of Deputies declared Versailles a museum. A restoration of the complex was undertaken after World War I, underwritten by Rockefeller, and was continued by the French government after 1952. Today, the palace's halls and salons recount their magical history, which is rendered all the more exceptional by some breathtaking figures: a surface area of 1,976 acres; 330,000 plants; 375 windows facing

117 *Glimpses of the interior of the palace bear witness to the magnificence of the decorations completed for Louis XIV, his successor Louis XV, the only king to have spent his life and the years of his reign at Versailles, and Louis XVI. In the royal chapel, dedicated to St. Louis (center) the harmony of the neoclassical colonnade stands out. The staircase that leads to the apartments of the queen (bottom right), features beautiful inlaid marble, and the Galerie des Batailles (top right), created in 1836 in the old apartments of the southern wing, is an important picture gallery containing works depicting the great battles. The pictures now belong to the Musée de l'Histoire de France, which was established in the 19th century.*

118 left
Gold is the central motif in the splendors of the royal palace. In this photograph is a detail of the decoration of the paneling designed by Richard Mique in 1783 for the queen's Cabinet Doré.

118 top
The interiors of the Palace of Versailles are clear evidence of the boundless luxury of the king's apartments. Particularly fine rooms are the Salon de l'Oeil de Boeuf (left) and Marie-Antoinette's chamber (right).

118–119 *It was in this sumptuous room that King Louis XIV, the Sun King, died in 1715. Elegant gilded friezes, brocades, and precious tapestries are features of what was from 1701 the king's bedchamber. The ceremony of the* lever du Roi *took place in this room each morning as the members of the royal family and the courtiers paid homage to the sovereign.*

119 *While it took half a century to construct the Palace of Versailles for the Sun King, it took a further 20 years, different kings, and much work to bring it to the pitch of magnificence enjoyed by all those who pass through the gilded entrance gates today. In this photograph can be seen the queen's chamber, which was decorated by two famous masters, Jacques and Jacques Ange Gabriel, during the reign of Louis XV. The chamber is preceded by an antechamber known as the* Grand Couvert, *which has with a heavily decorated ceiling.*

onto the enormous garden; and 70 gardeners, 200 guards, 12 firemen, and 400 members of the general staff to maintain the "factory of marvels." The palace receives nearly 5 million visitors each year.

During the king's tenure at the palace, rigorous order was imposed: The princes and other dignitaries lived in the north and the south wings, facing the garden, and the courtiers had their apartments by the village. The royal apartments are on the first floor of the main building—the king to the north, and the queen to the south. They were reached via two marble staircases, that of the ambassadors, which no longer exists, and that of the queen. Behind the Cour des Ministres, bounded by balustrades and featuring an equestrian statue of Louis XIV and memories of Montgolfier and Pilâtre de Rozier's early ballooning experiments, lies the Royal Court, which only the carriages of the royal family and ministers reached. The Cour de Marbre follows, with its traces of the original castle of Louis XIII, and the king's bed chamber at the center. The Opéra, a building constructed in just one year (1770) for the wedding of Louis XVI and Marie-Antoinette of Austria, is architect Gabriel's masterpiece.

The western facade of the palace, which is accessed via the Cour Royale, extends a full 1,900 feet. Inside are rooms dedicated to Louis XIII and Louis XIV, with portraits of

kings, queens, court favorites and famous people. Also here is the grand apartment of the monarch, composed of six ceremonial rooms, and the Hall of Mirrors—Versailles at its most theatrical. The hall was created by Mansart from 1678 to 1686 and is decorated with paintings by Le Brun. Today the 17 panels mirrored with mercury, illuminated by as many windows, reflect the figures of visitors, but during the time of the Sun King, they reflected a roomful of precious furniture of pure silver set against the walls of the long gallery. Other apartments with the bedchambers of the various kings that lived in the palace and salons filled with treasures, silk tapestries, and famous paintings lead to the offices of Louis XV, masterpieces of French decorative art and cabinetmaking. Other noteworthy highlights

121 top left *Louis XIV kept and admired the masterpieces in his art collection, such as the* Mona Lisa, *in small, private apartments. The photograph shows the Cabinet de la Pendule, which owes its name to the astronomical clock in the background.*

121 top right *Official life of the court took place in the great apartments. This is the Salon du Mercure. Beginning with the Salon du Hercule, each apartment is dedicated to a Greek divinity.*

120 *This small theater was built for Marie-Antoinette toward the end of the 18th century and is in the gardens of the Grand Trianon.*

include the queen's apartments, the room of the queen's guard, the coronation hall, the apartment of the dauphine and dauphin, and then, after the long tour of power and luxury, the silence of the immense park.

The park's fountains run from May to September on scheduled Sundays and attract up to 20,000 visitors a day to marvel at the play of the myriad water features. Also during the summer months are the great night parties that evoke, at Neptune's Pool, the spectacular celebrations at the time of the Sun King.

120–121 *Louis XVI had the Grand Trianon, a sumptuous palace in stone and pink marble, built in 1687 as a refuge from the strict court protocol. This is the Salon des Glaces, the hall in which the king received his ministers and the members of the royal family.*

To the right of the Grand Canal, inside the park, is the Grand Trianon, the work of Le Vau, erected on acres of former pastures and villages that were destroyed to make room for the *bon plaisir du roi*. The Grand Trianon stunned contemporary observers: "a nothing, just a small thing crouched between flowers, jasmine, oranges, intimate and splendid." This ceramic *rêverie*, entirely covered in white and blue porcelain, was a secluded refuge where the king and queen could repose in intimacy. Today, the ceramic has been replaced by white and pink marble, reestablishing the Grand Trianon as a masterpiece of refinement.

The *hameau de la reine* was constructed on the banks of an artificial lake for Marie-Antoinette. The building was a life-size puppet theater, inspired by Jean-Jacques Rousseau's call for a return to nature. Nested in the greenery not far away is the Petit Trianon, five sumptuously furnished rooms and a beautiful English-style garden with magnificent exotic and rare trees. The cottage was a favorite of Marie- Antoinette's, before that, it was the last residence of Madame de Pompadour, the king's lover.

122–123 *The Galerie des Glaces in the Palace of Versailles is illuminated by 17 great windows that throw light onto an equal number of arched mirrors. Scenes depicting episodes from the life of Louis XIV were painted on the ceiling by Le Brun.*

INDEX

c=caption

T

U

V

W

Y

Z

ILLUSTRATION CREDITS

Cover: *Marcello Bertinetti / Archivio White Star*
Back cover:
Marcello Bertinetti / Archivio White Star: top left, center bottom left.
Giulio Veggi / Archivio White Star: top center, top right, center top left, center bottom left, center top right, center bottom right, bottom right.
Photo Nimatallah / Agenzia Luisa Ricciarini: bottom left.

Marcello Bertinetti / Archivio White Star: pages 56–57, 59 left, 60–61, 61 top, 76 bottom, 79 top left, 92 bottom, 92–93, 100 top and bottom, 102 bottom left, 102 top right, 108, 108–109, 110 bottom, 112–113, 128.
Luciano Ramires / Archivio White Star: pages 66–67, 87, 104 bottom left, 104 right.
Giulio Veggi / Archivio White Star: pages 1, 6–7, 55 top, 56 top, 56 left, 57 top, 59 right, 60 left, 62 left, 62 top, 62–63, 64 top, 65, 68–69, 70, 74, 75, 78, 80 top, 81 right, 90 top, 91, 92 top, 97 bottom, 98–99, 99, 101 top, 102 top and center left, 102 bottom right, 105, 106 top, 109 top, 110 top.
AKG Photo: pages 23 right, 24 bottom right, 33 top and bottom, 35 bottom left and bottom right, 36 bottom left, 37, 39 top and center, 47 bottom, 50 top left, 50–51, 51 top, 52.
Archivio Scala: pages 21 bottom left, 25 top right, 31 bottom left, 49 bottom, 63 top right, 89 top right.
Barnaby's Picture Library: page 51 center right.
Yann Arthus Bertrand / Altitude / The Image Bank: pages 12–13, 55 bottom, 79 top right, 80–81, 84–85, 93 top, 97 top, 99 top left, 114–115.
Foto BIP / Agenzia Luisa Ricciarini: pages 61 bottom, 99 top right.
Stefano Cellai / Sie: page 86.
Jean Marc Charles / Agenzia Franca Speranza: pages 78–79.
J.M. Charles / Rapho / Grazia Neri: page 111 top.
Jean Loup Charmet: pages 19 right, 25 bottom, 38 top, 42, 43, 44–45, 45 center, 46 center, 47 center.
Gian Carlo Costa / Agenzia Stradella: pages 23 top left, 41 bottom, 48 bottom.
Marco Cristofori / SIE: page 83.
Giovanni Dagli Orti: pages 16 top, 16–17, 18 bottom, 19 left, 20 center left, 20 bottom, 22 top right, 24 left, 26, 28 top, 29 top and bottom, 30 top, 30–31, 31 top, 31 bottom right, 32 left, 32 bottom, 34 top, 36–37, 44 top left, 45 top and bottom, 46–47, 49 top and center, 63 top left, 85, 94 top, 94–95, 114, 115 top, 116, 117, 118, 119, 120, 121, 122–123.
R. De Pardon / Gamma: page 53 bottom right.
E.T. Archive: pages 35 top, 47 top, 55 top left and right, 72, 73 center left, 73 bottom right.
Mary Evans Picture Library: page 50 bottom.
Fototeca Storica Nazionale: pages 17 top, 18 top, 22 top left, 28 bottom right, 48 top right, 50 top right.
Sylvain Grandadam: pages 64 bottom, 82 bottom.
Johanna Huber / SIME: page 4.
M.J. Jarry / J.F. Tripelon / Agence Top / Grazia Neri: pages 77, 103, 104 top left, 107.
Photo Nimatallah / Agenzia Luisa Ricciarini: pages 21 top, 71 bottom left, 73 top, 73 center right, 73 bottom left.
Andrea Pistolesi: pages 6 left, 54 top, 76 top, 82 top.
Private Collection: pages 16 center and bottom, 20 top and center right, 21 bottom right, 22–23, 25 top left, 27 bottom left, 29 center, 48 top and center.
J.P. Rey / Gamma: page 53 top and center.
Agenzia Luisa Ricciarini: pages 27 top right, 32–33, 33 center, 34 bottom, 35 center right, 44 top right, 50 center left, 71 bottom right, 88, 89 bottom right, 94 bottom.
Ripani / SIME: page 76 left.
Schinco / Focus Team: pages 106–107.
Giovanni Simeone / SIME: pages 8–9, 10–11, 54–55, 90–91, 96 top, 96–97, 100–101.
Emilio F. Simion, Agenzia Luisa Ricciarini: pages 40 top right, 89 top left and bottom.
Harald Sund / The Image Bank: pages 2–3.
Pascal Tournaire: page 5.
Gilbert Uzan / Gamma: page 53 center bottom.
Viouiard / Gamma: page 53 bottom left.
Hans Wolf / The Image Bank: pages 110–111.

136 *The warm embrace of the setting sun and the car headlights frame the Arc de Triomphe.*